COGAT
KINDERGARTEN

Content:

Overview of *CogAT* for Parents

What is the *Cognitive Abilities Test*™ (*CogAT®*)?

The term "cognitive ability" describes a student's capacity to learn in a variety of contexts and settings and exhibit original problem-solving techniques. A child's ability to reason abstractly and recognize patterns and correlations in their environment is measured by the Cognitive Abilities Test (CogAT), as opposed to a typical achievement test, which gauges how well a student has mastered the curriculum.

Verbal, nonverbal, and quantitative reasoning are the three domains, or batteries, in which the CogAT assesses reasoning. These domains are based on the key ways that students and teachers interact in the classroom.The kinds of items contained in each CogAT battery are depicted in Figure 1. A representative item from each subtest (second grade level) is displayed in Figure 2.

Figure 1

Types of Reasoning Assessed

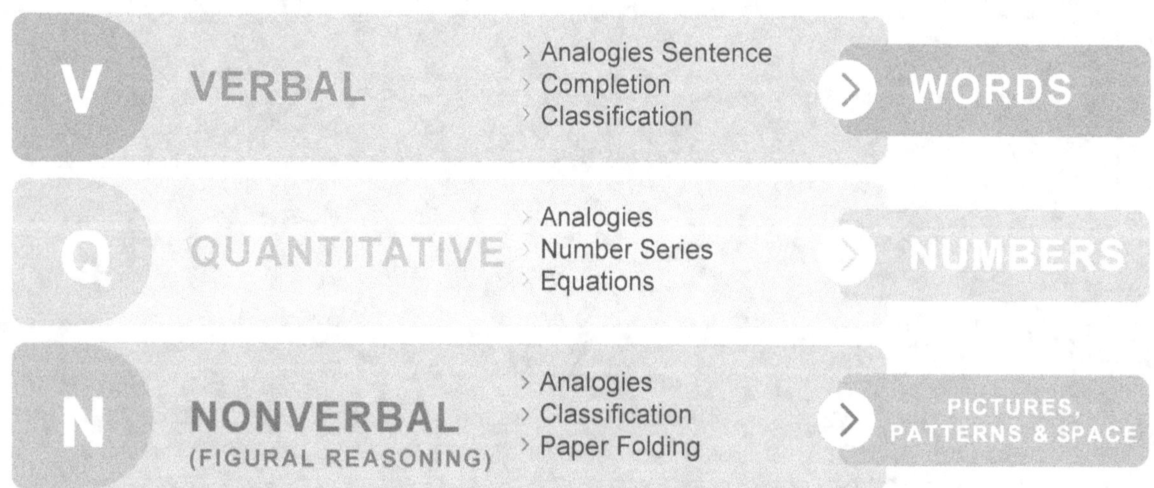

Verbal – Picture Analogies

Verbal – Picture Classification

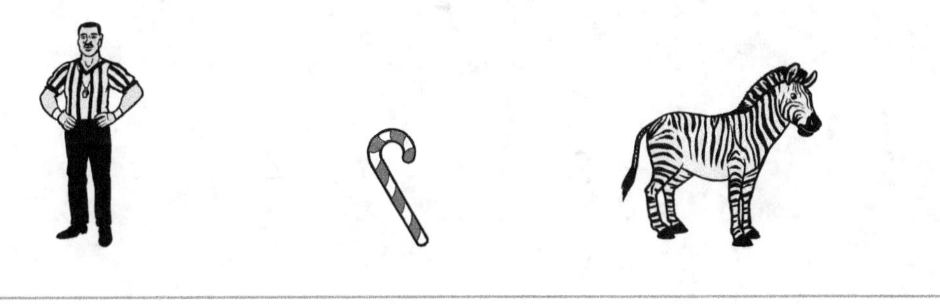

Verbal – Sentence Completion (not pictured)

Quantitative – Number Analogies

1 

Quantitative – Number Puzzles

2   3   4   6

Quantitative – Number Series

5

Nonverbal – Figure Matrices

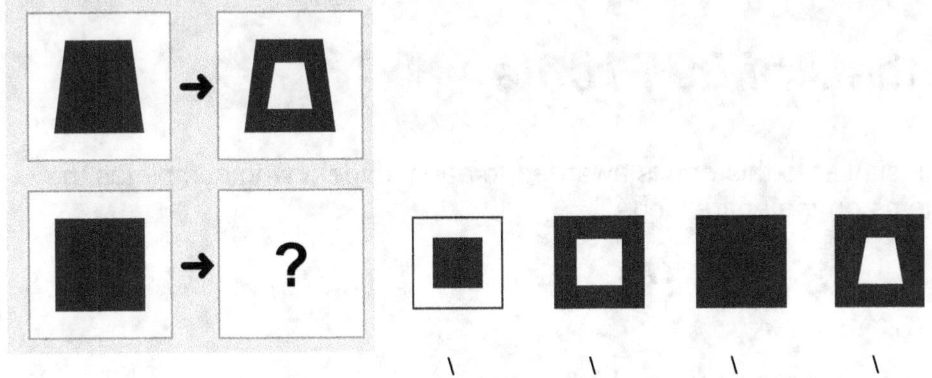

Nonverbal – Figure Classification

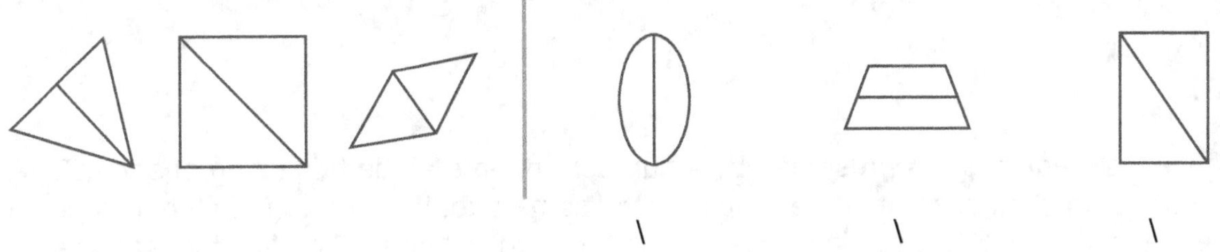

Nonverbal – Paper Folding

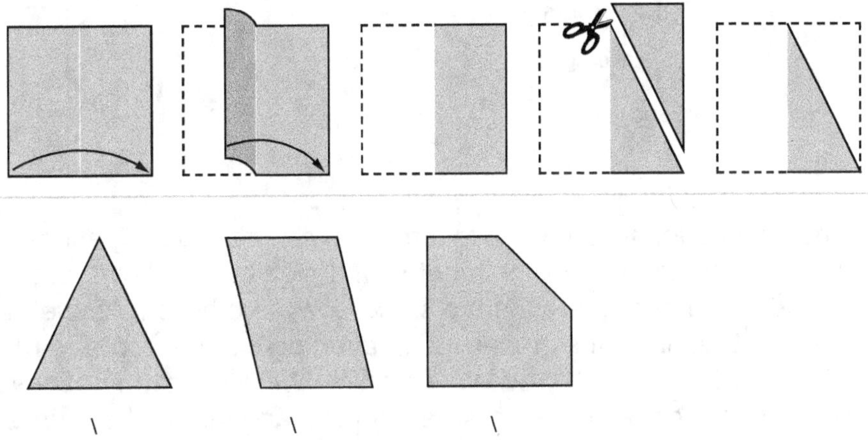

Each student obtains an Ability Profile—a brief code that encapsulates their cognitive abilities —after completing the entire CogAT. This guide will help you comprehend ability data and how to use it, as well as how to interpret the Ability Profile.

Interpreting the *Ability Profile*

An Ability Profile code similar to this one is awarded to each student who completes the required amount of items on the entire CogAT:

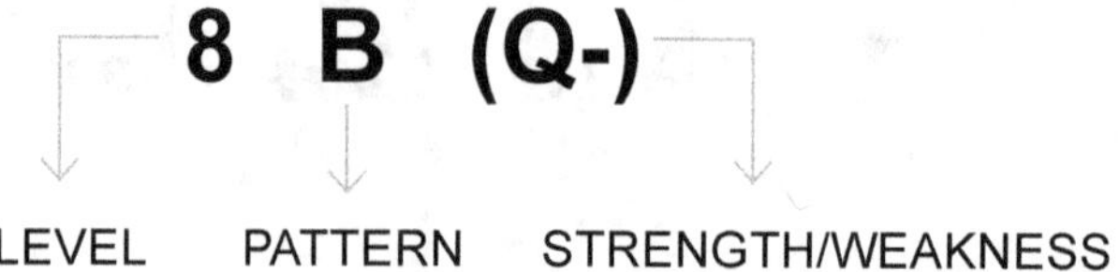

With the use of this Ability Profile, educators may better cater to the requirements of their students, help parents better support their kids at home, and provide students a deeper grasp of their own learning. The interpretation of each section of the profile is explained in the following sections.

Level

The student's median age represented by a number appears at the beginning of each CogAT Ability Profile. In comparison to other pupils of the same age, this shows the student's general degree of thinking ability. "Standard nine" is shortened to "stanine." The fact that stanine scores vary from a low of 1 to a high of 9 is where the name originates.

Interpreting Stanine Level

Level	Indication
1, 2, 3	below average
4, 5, 6	average
7, 8	above average
9	very high

The test computes scores using a national sample of test results, referred to as "national norms". Students between the ages of four years and eleven months and eighteen and over are grouped by age every month. Your child performed at around the same level as other pupils their age who took the test, according to the test results if they received an average stanine score (4-6). A youngster outperformed other test-takers if they receive a stanine score of seven or above, which is above average. A child's performance on the exam was poorer than that of other pupils their age if their stanine score was below average (1-3). For a graphic illustration, see to Figure 3:

Median Stanine by Reasoning Ability Level

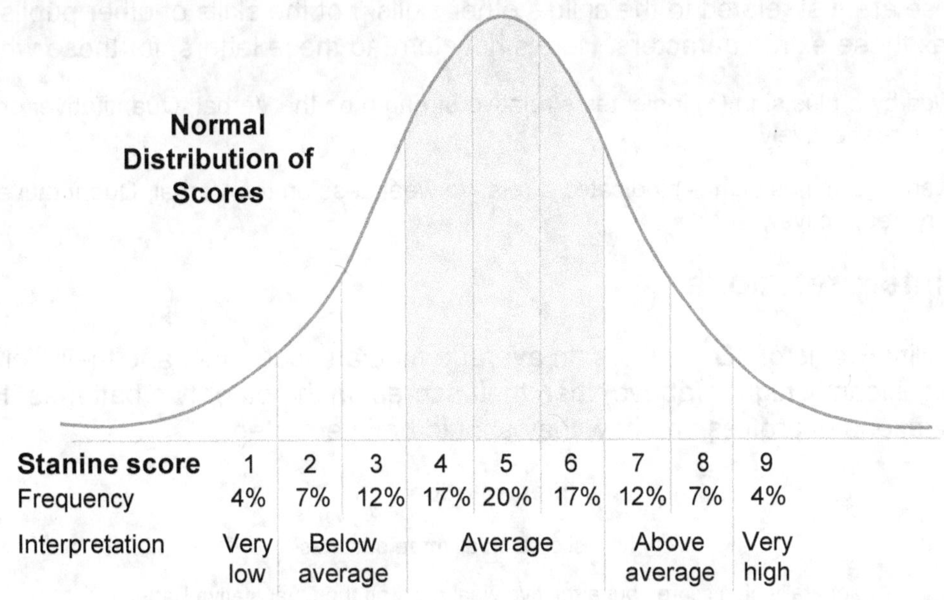

Pattern

A letter that represents the scoring pattern for your child comes after the median score. The pattern indicates whether there is a substantial difference in some of the three battery results or whether they are all roughly equal. A, B, C, or E profiles can be applied to the pattern.

Pattern	Description	Approximate percentage of students with this profile
A	The student's Verbal, Quantitative, and Nonverbal Battery scores are roughly at the sAme level	44%
B	Two of the scores are roughly the same. The third score is a relative strength or weakness, significantly aBove or Below the other two.	33%
C	Two scores Contrast. The student shows a relative strength and a relative weakness.	12%
E	An E profile indicates Extreme score differences. At least two scores differ by 24 or more points on the standard age score (SAS) scale.	10%

Relative strengths and weaknesses

Following the pattern, there might be one or two more letters that represent the student's relative strengths and/or weaknesses as shown by their battery scores, depending on their Ability Profile. Remember that these are just related to the child's other skills, not the skills of other pupils. Not every profile has these extra characters. Here's how to read these letters, for those who do:

- V, Q, or N followed by a plus sign (+) indicates a relative strength on the Verbal, Quantitative, or Nonverbal Battery, respectively.

- V, Q, or N followed by a minus sign (–) indicates a relative weakness on the Verbal, Quantitative, or Nonverbal Battery, respectively.

Sample score interpretations

A student with an Ability Profile of 4B (V+) has an average median score of 4, and their Verbal Battery result was significantly higher (above) than their scores on the other two batteries. Here are some more illustrations of profiles and how they should be interpreted:

Profile	Interpretation
9A	Very high scores on all three batteries
8B (Q-)	Generally high scores but a relative weakness on the Quantitative Battery
2B (N+)	Generally below average scores, but a relative strength on the Nonverbal Battery
5C (V+N-)	Generally average scores with a relative strength on the Verbal Battery and a relative weakness on the Nonverbal Battery
8E (V-)	Generally high scores but an extreme relative weakness on the Verbal Battery

How can ability data **be used**?

A special and effective tool that tells parents, teachers, and students about a student's potential is the Ability Profile.

Teachers can arrange students with people who will complement and enhance their learning and modify lessons based on best practices for each ability level using the information from the profile. To promote academic progress, teachers can also employ focused techniques to build on pupils' unique strengths and help them strengthen their weaknesses. Students who are relatively strong in verbal reasoning, for instance, will gain from discussing or writing about what they are learning, whereas students who are stronger in nonverbal reasoning will gain from learning new concepts through the use of models and manipulatives. Rather than expecting a student who struggles with verbal reasoning to remember instructions, it could be more advantageous to write instructions on the board for them to refer to. When explaining math issues to a student who struggles with quantitative thinking, it is usually best to use illustrations and/or written explanations.

As parents, we can utilize this knowledge to help our kids learn and develop their critical thinking abilities at home. To make the most of the Ability Profile data, we invite you to review the Additional Resources listed below.

An important note about test scores

You child is a one-of-a-kind person with many incomparable personal traits and qualities that will shape what they bring to the world. You should know that the CogAT is just one test, and that results can be different based on many outside factors. It is still a great way to find out what our students are capable of. These results are a great way to see how well a student is doing in school, but they are not the only way to judge your child's skills and abilities. The school for your child uses a variety of tests, data, and notes to figure out what they need. If you want to help your child learn and reach their full potential, we hope that the Ability Profile will be useful to you and their teacher.

Non Verbal
Figure Clasification

Question 1

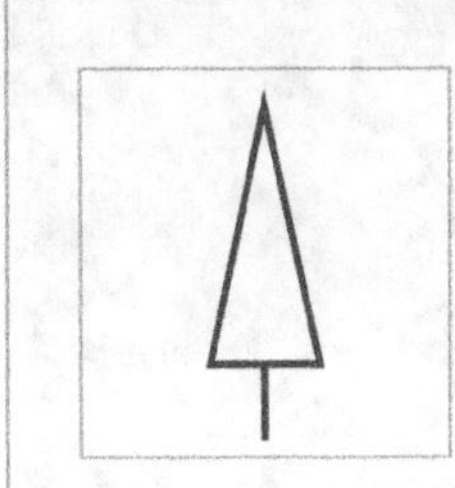 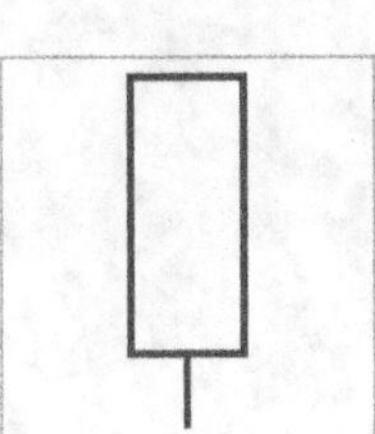 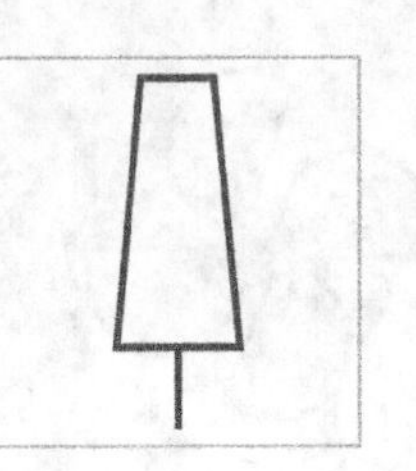

A 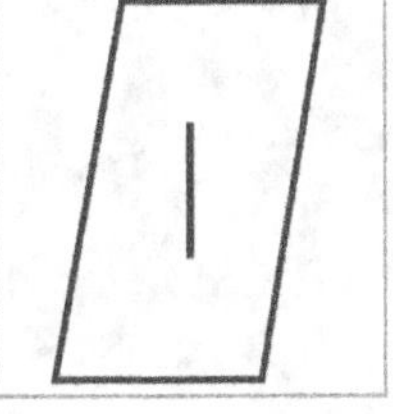

B 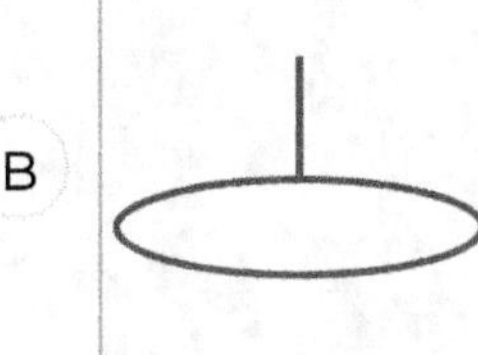

C 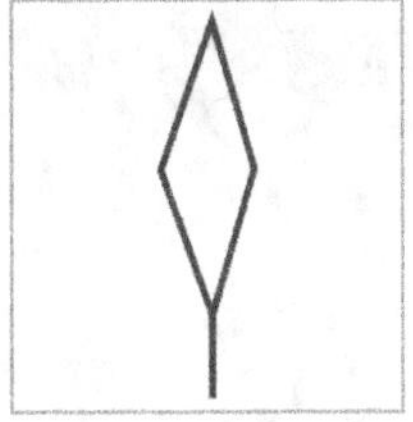

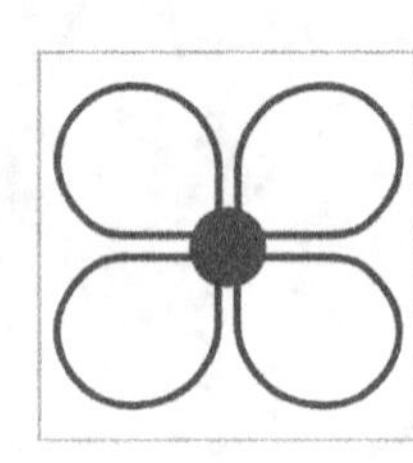  

A 

B 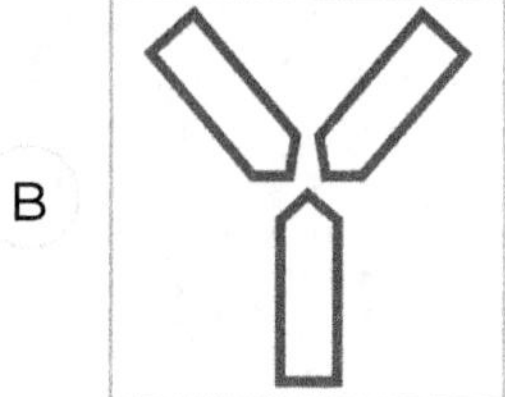

C 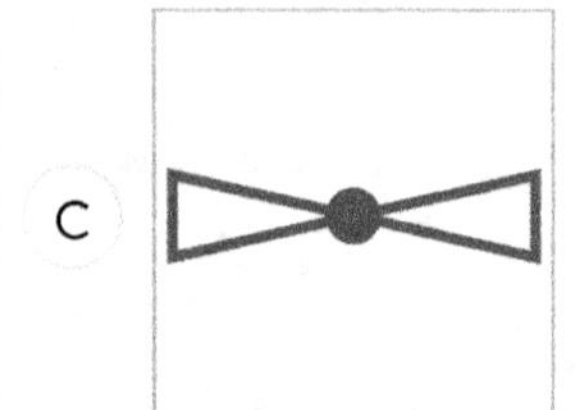

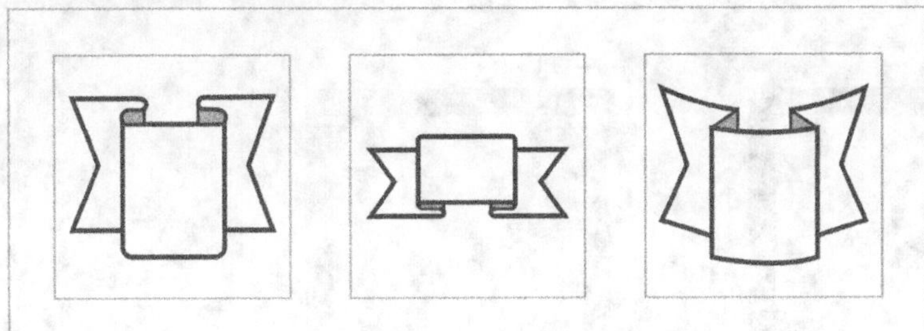

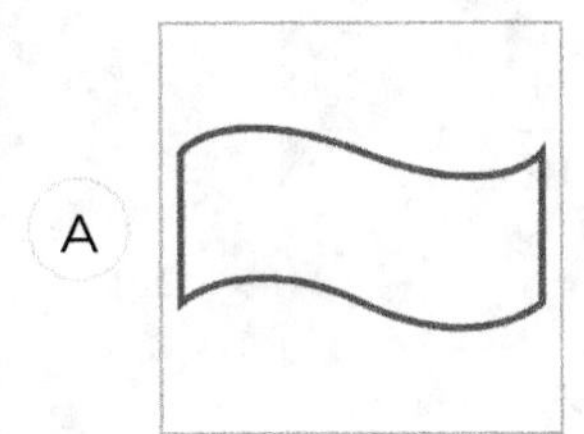

A

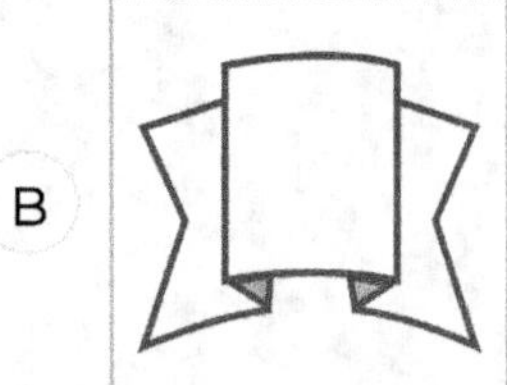

B

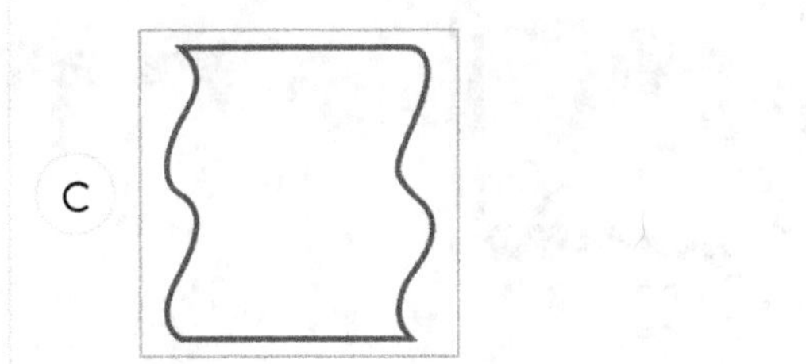

C

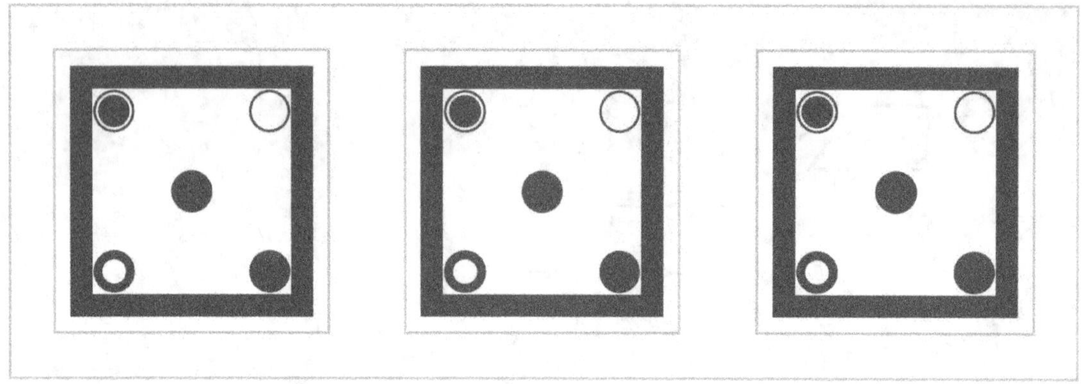

A 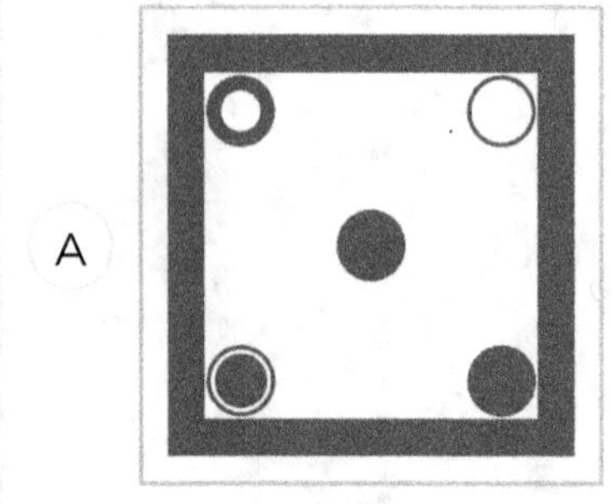

B 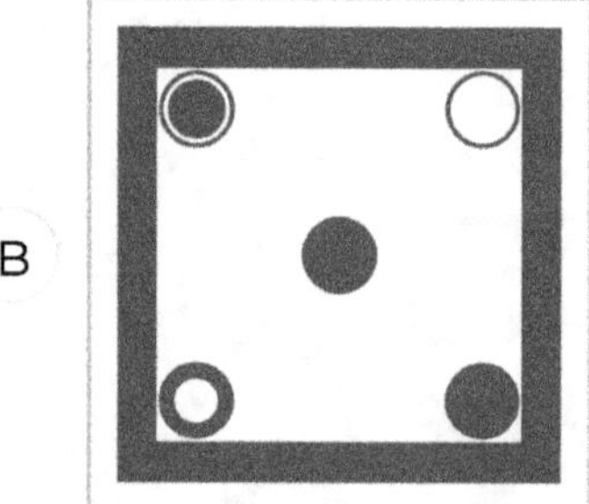

C 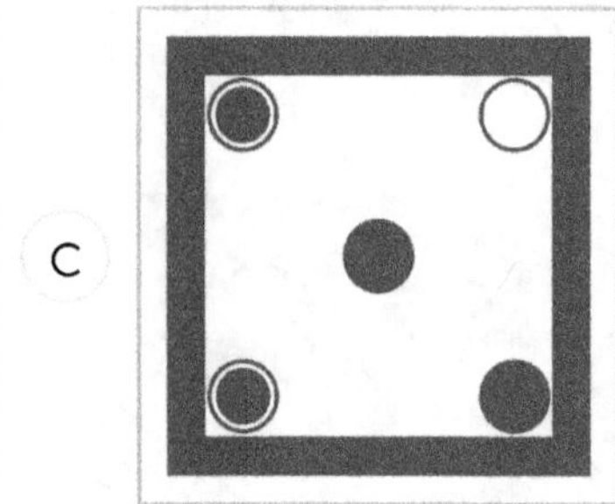

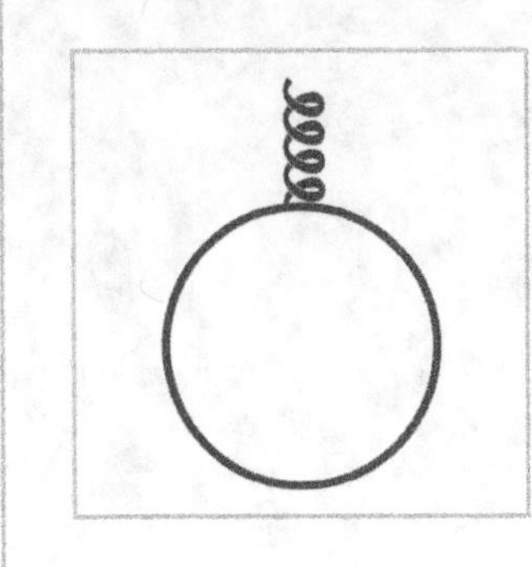 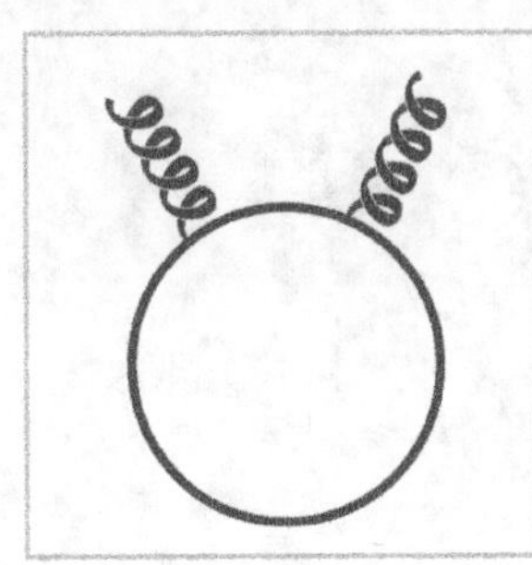 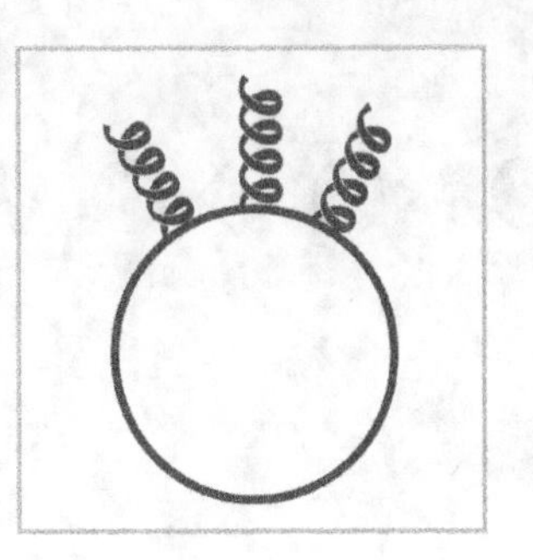

A

B 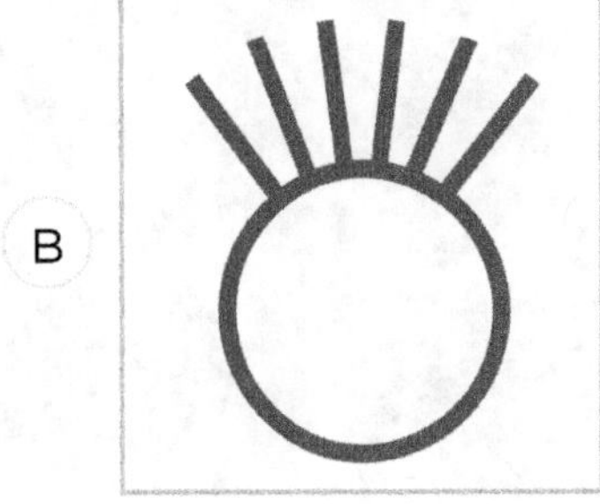

C

D 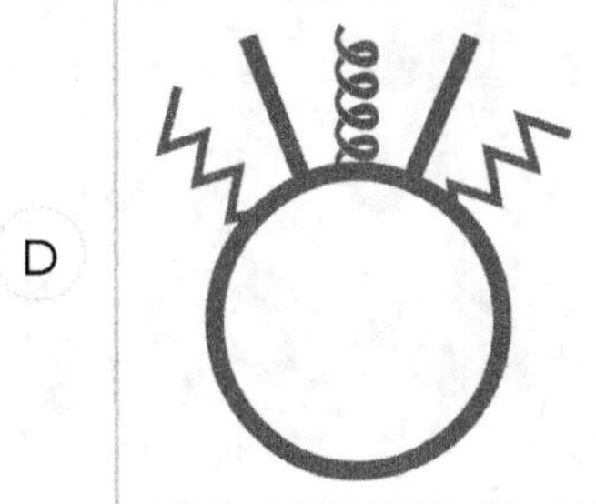

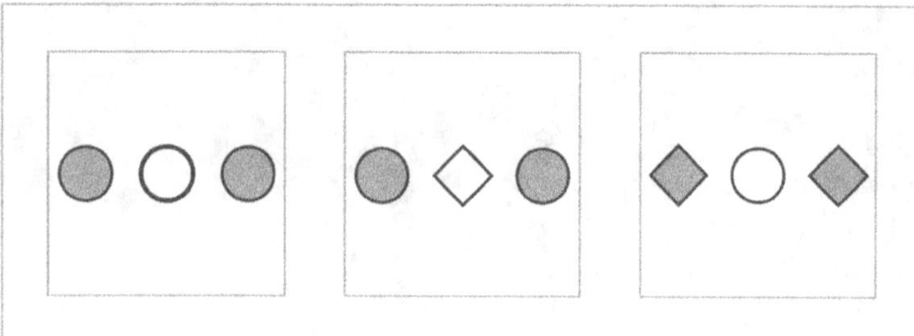

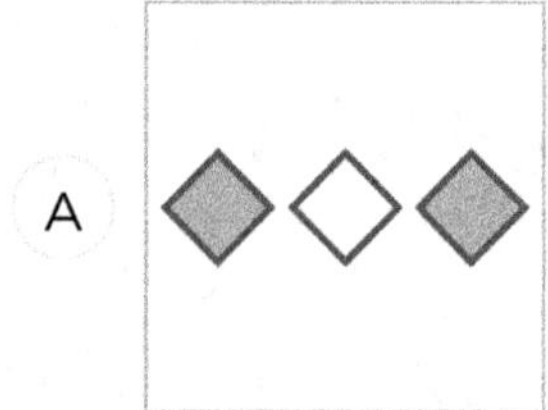

A

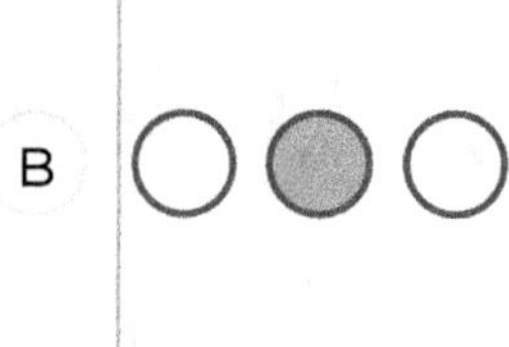

B

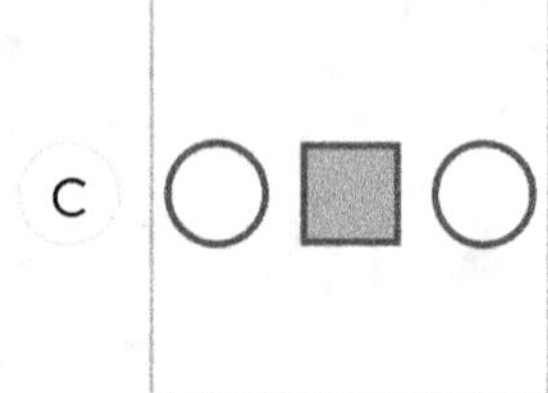

C

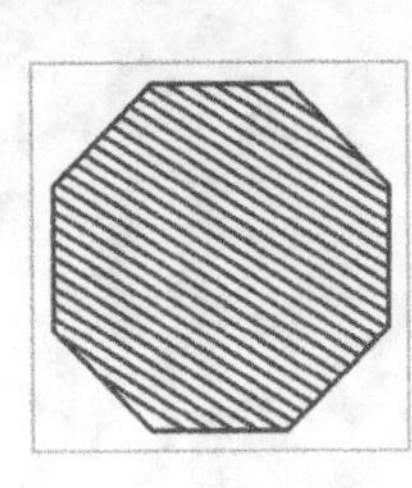 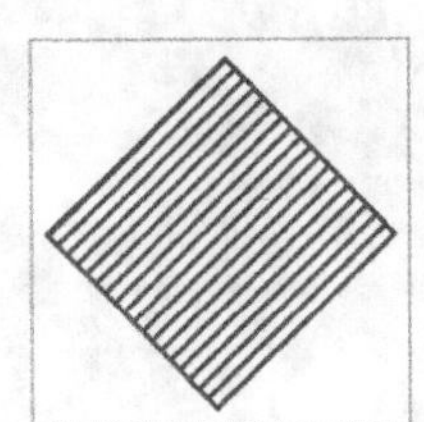 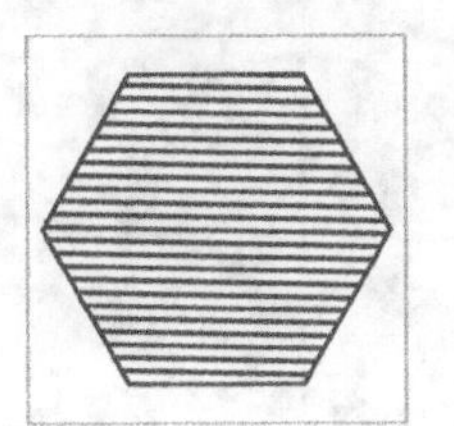

A 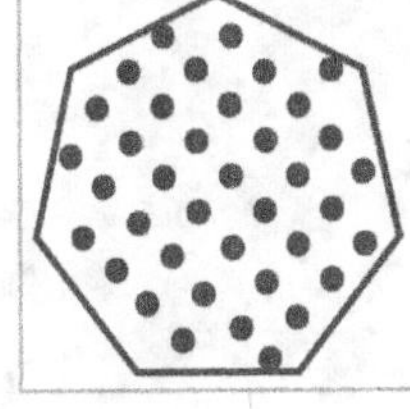

B 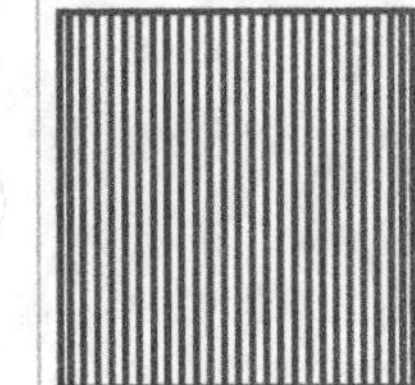

C 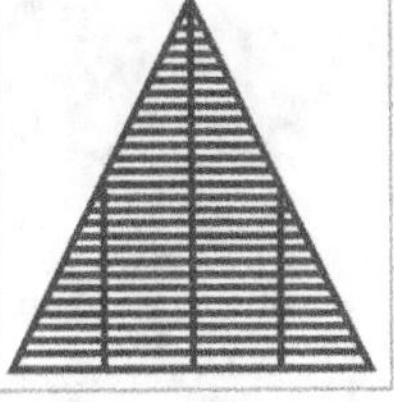

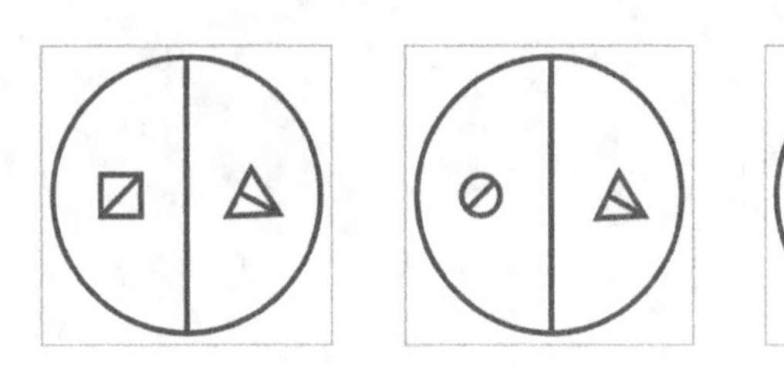

A 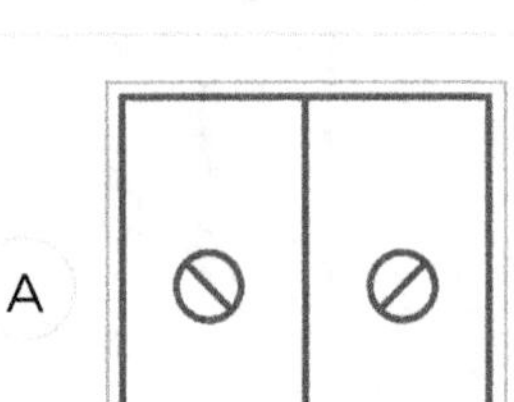

B 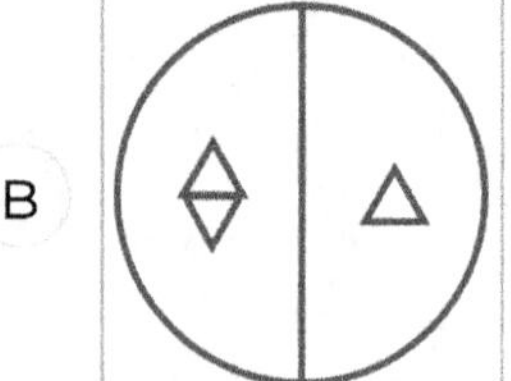

C

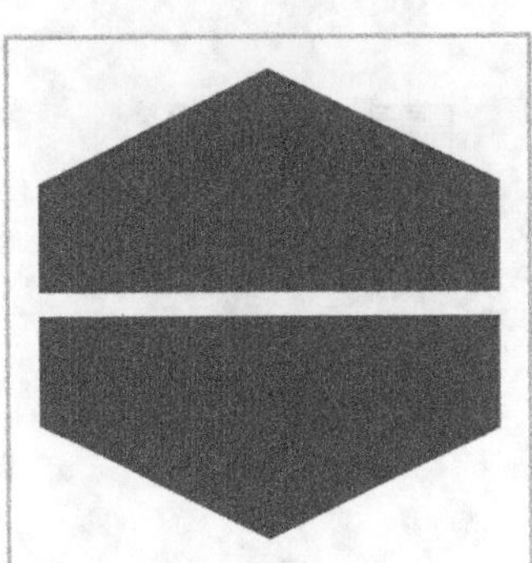
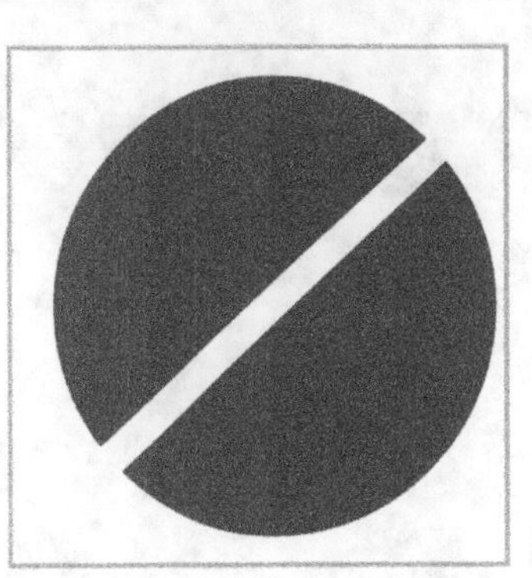

A
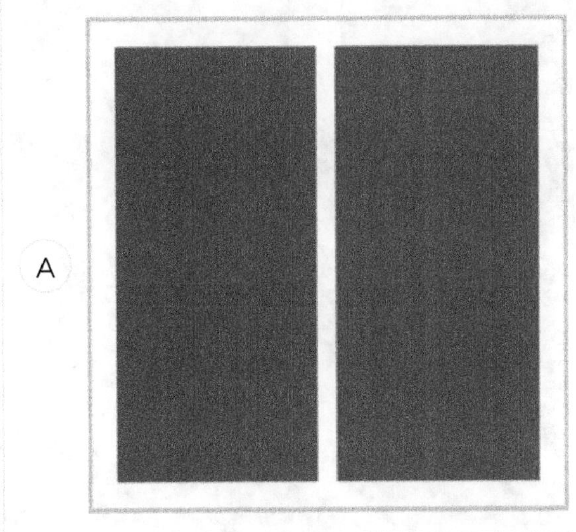

B
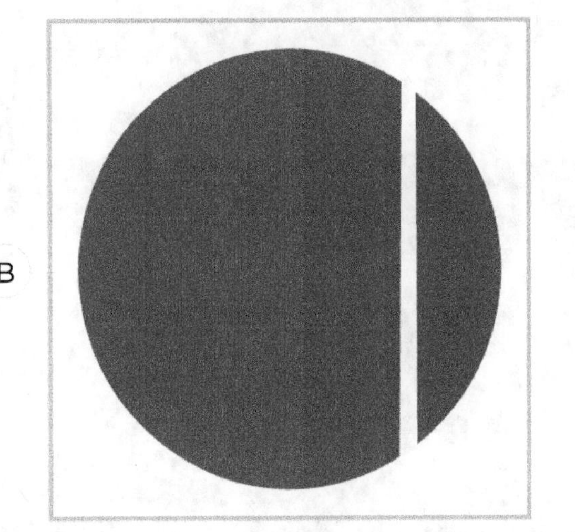

C
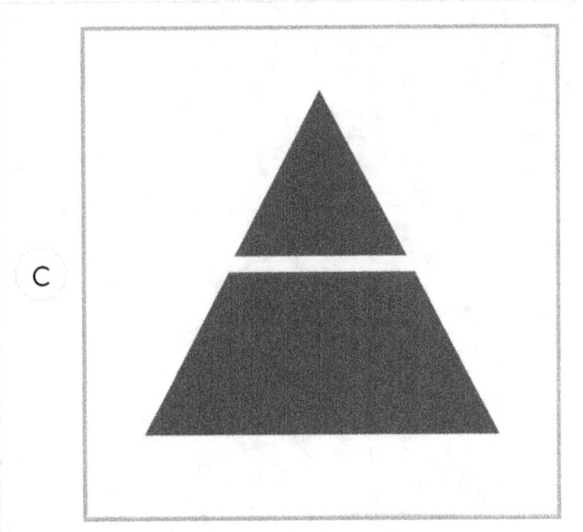

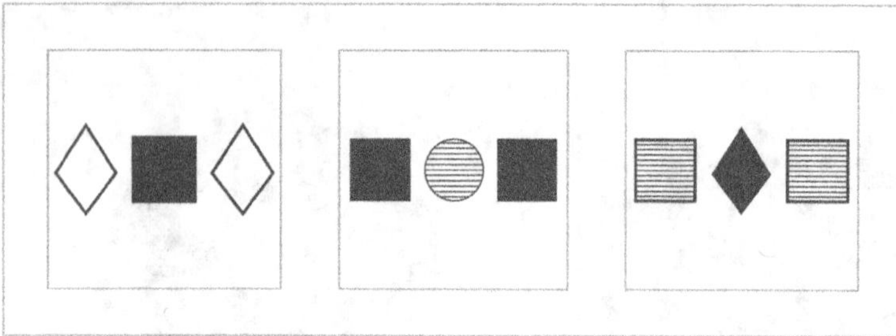

A
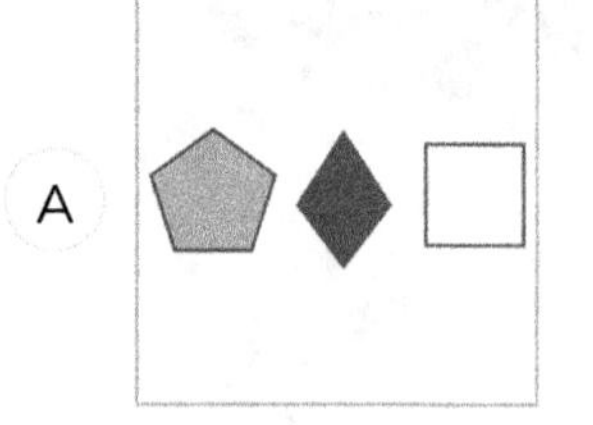

B
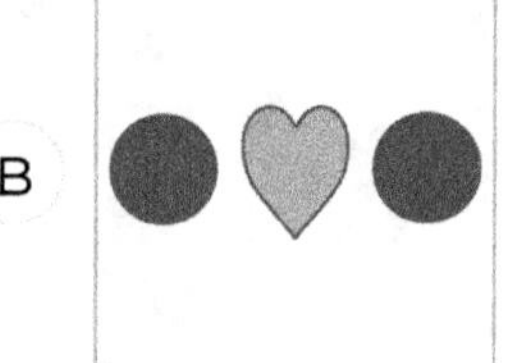

C
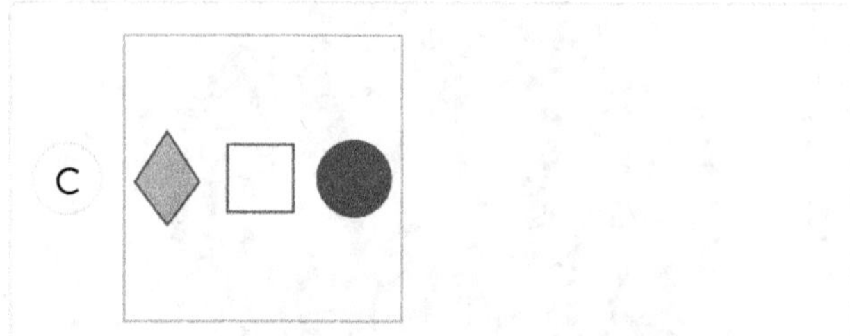

1. c
2. a
3. b
4. b
5. c
6. a
7. b
8. c
9. a
10. b

Non Verbal
Figure Matrices

Question 1

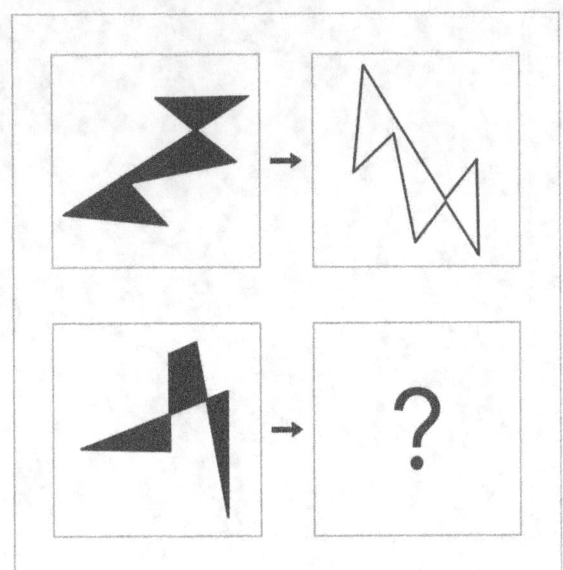

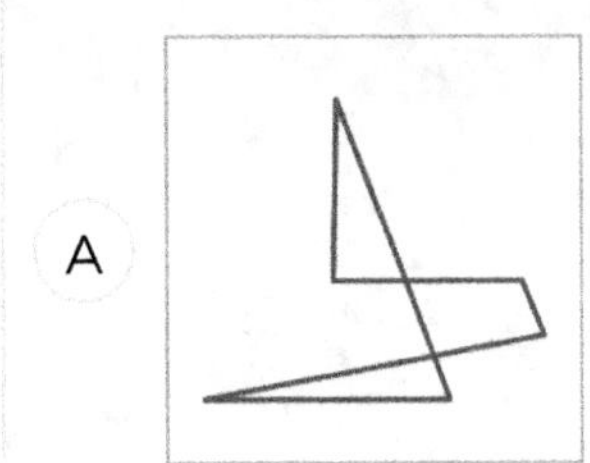

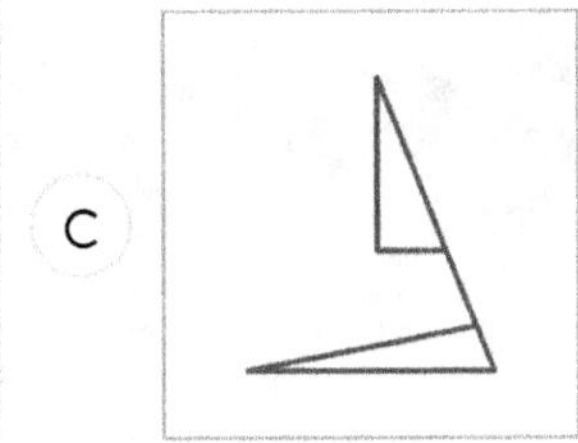

A

B

C

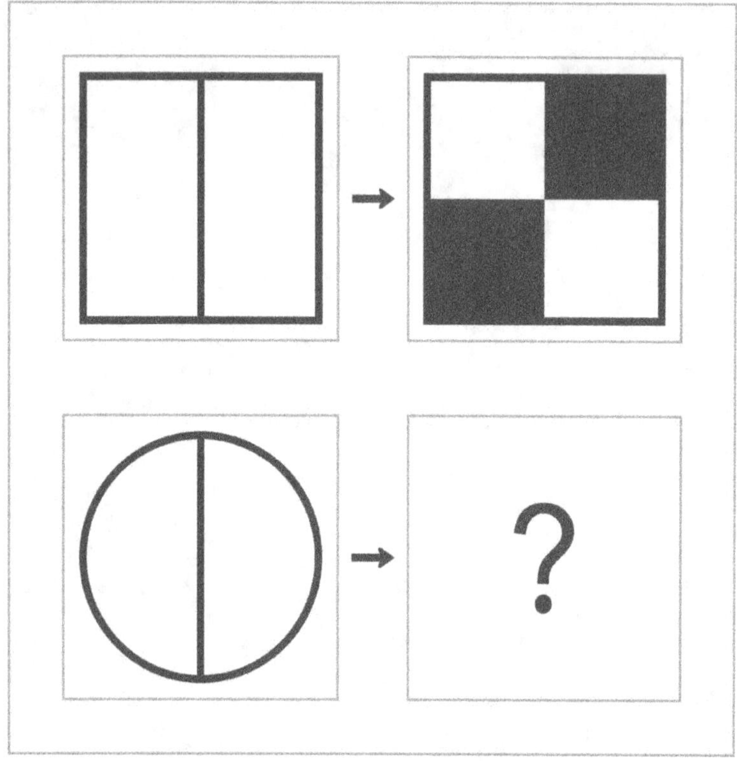

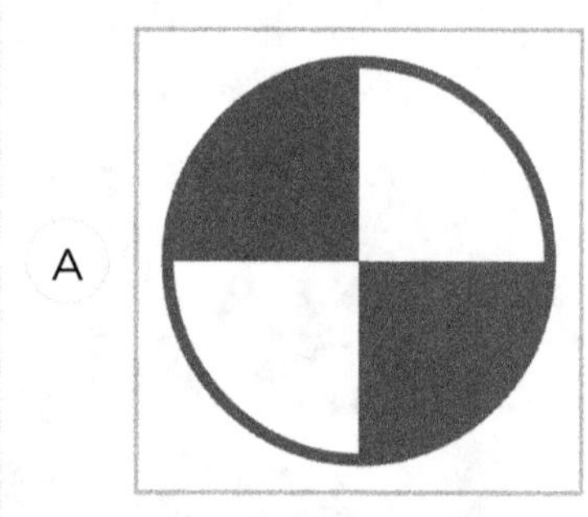

A

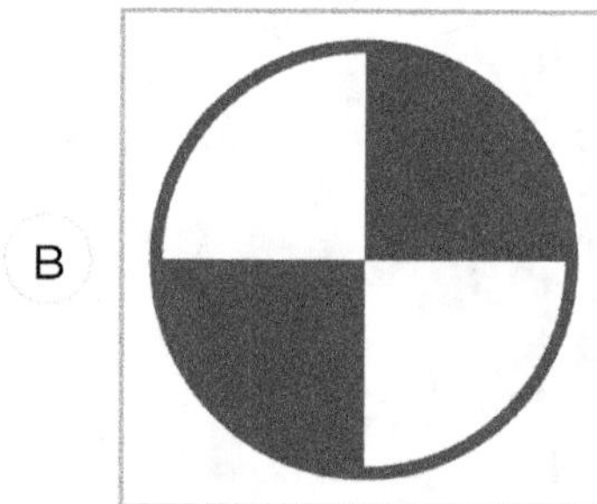

B

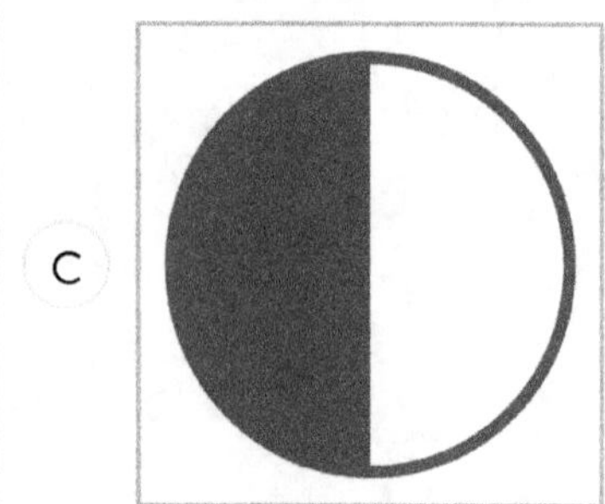

C

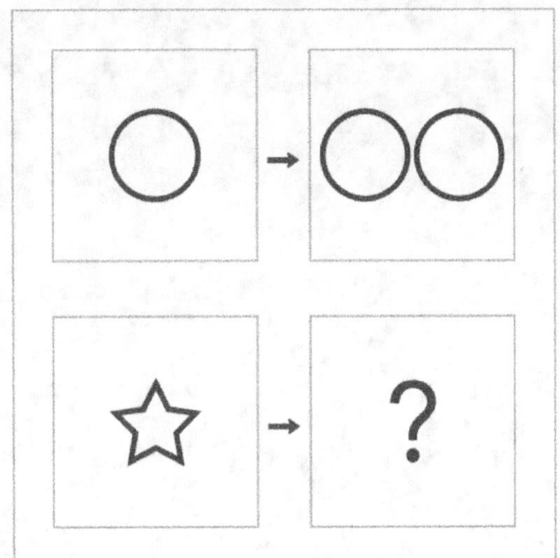

A 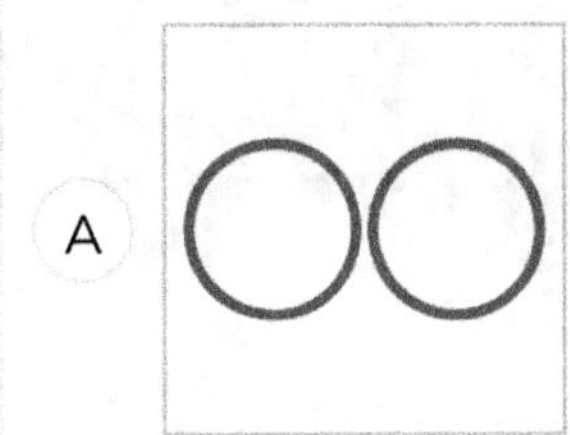

B 

C 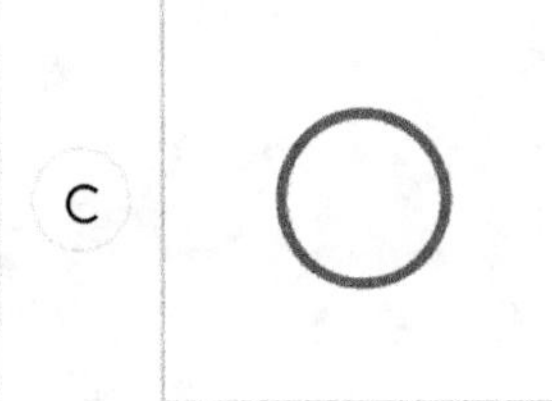

D 

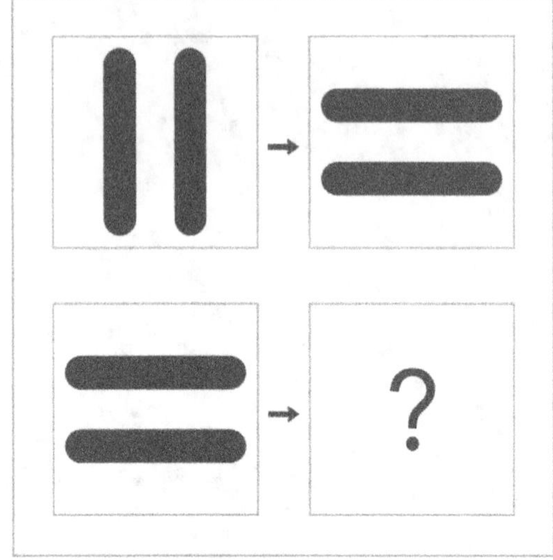

 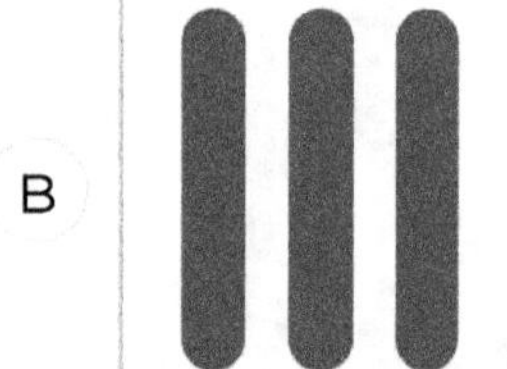

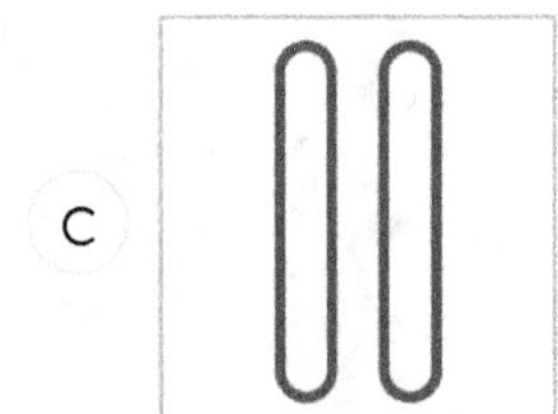 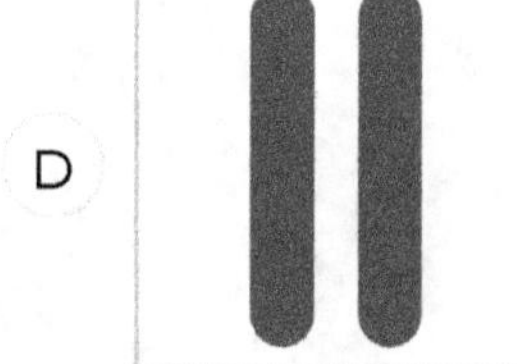

A

B

C

D

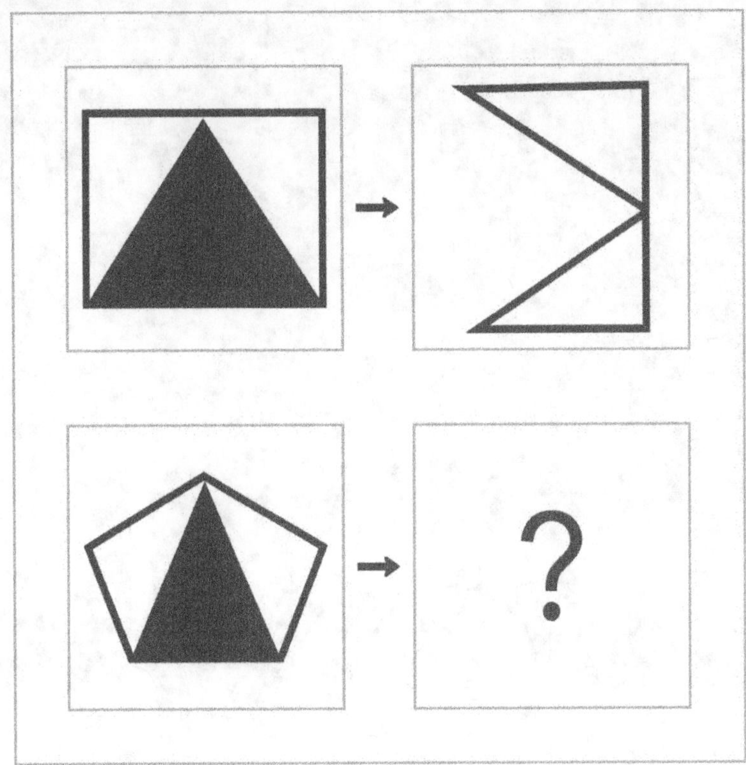

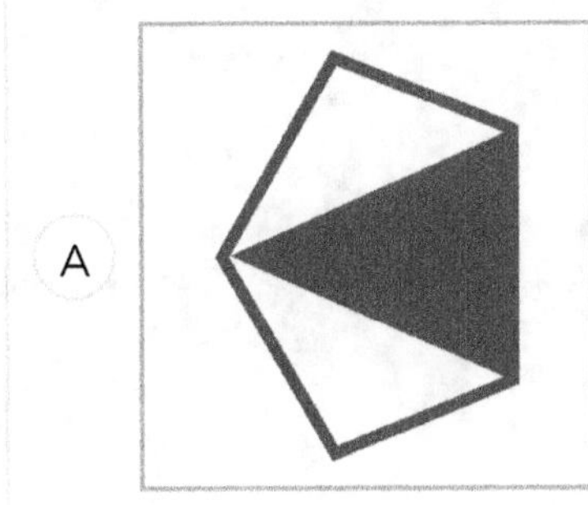

A

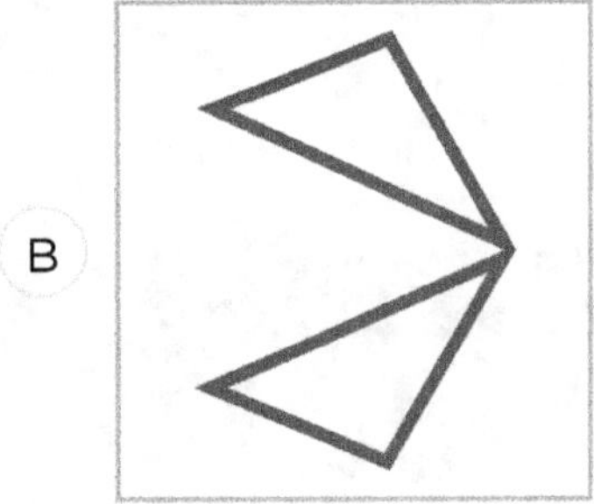

B

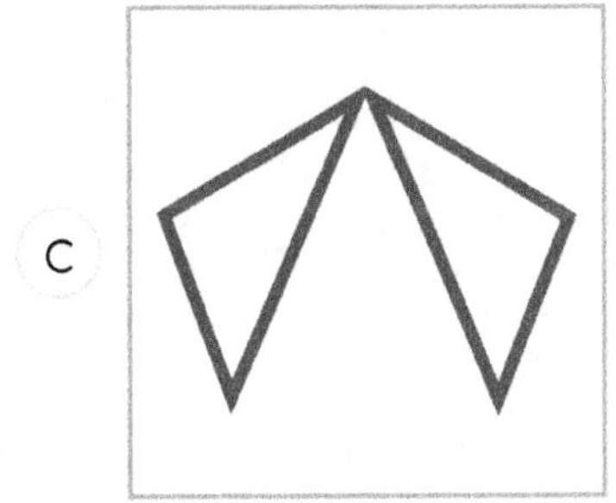

C

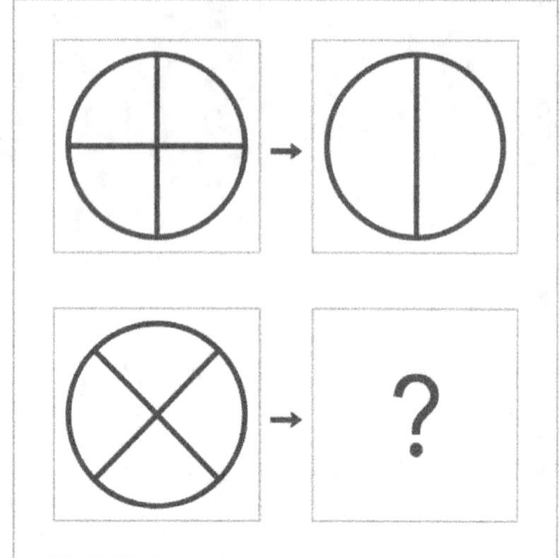

 → 

A 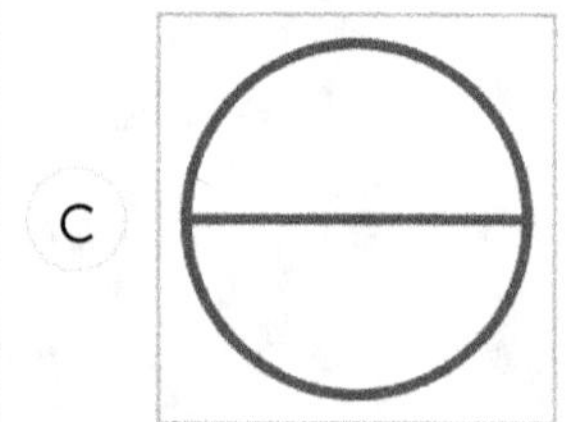

B

C

D 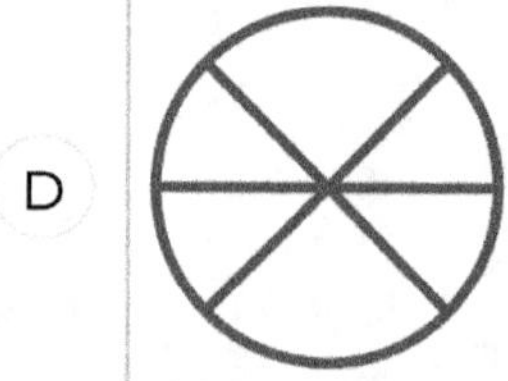

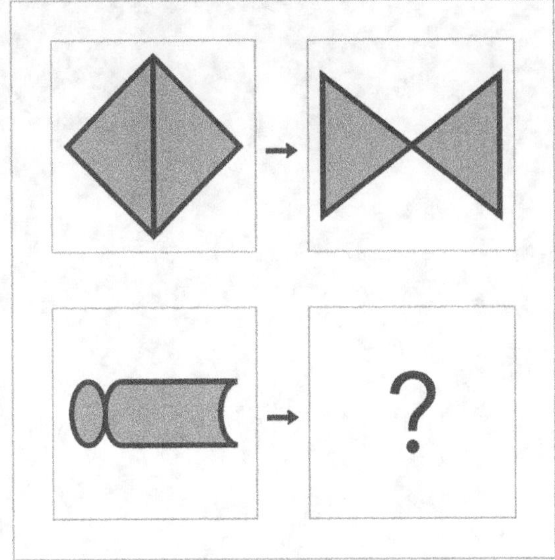

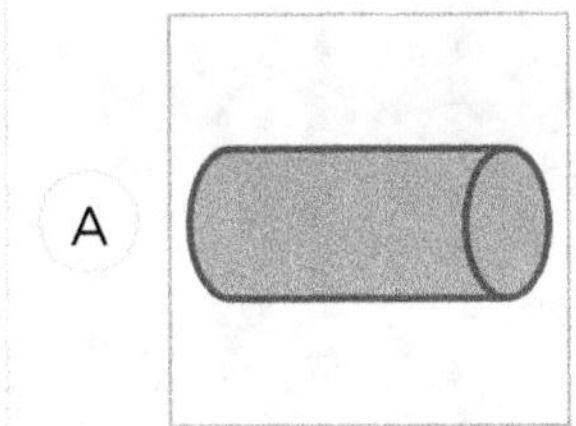

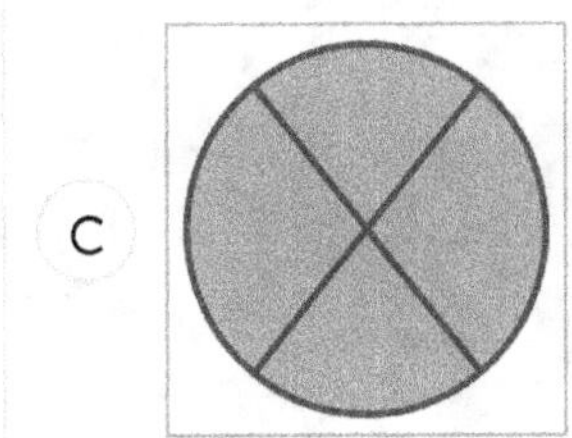

A

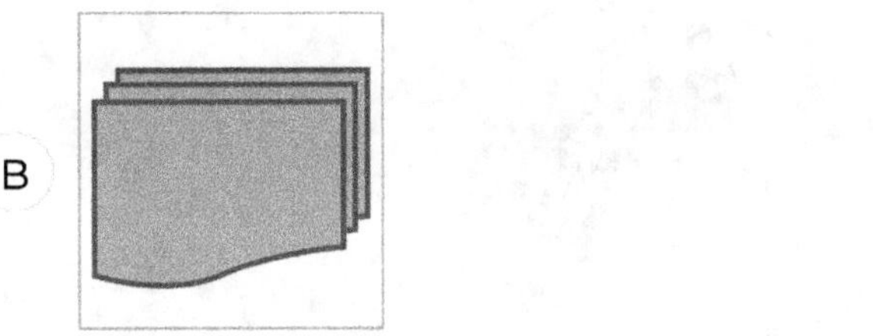

B

C

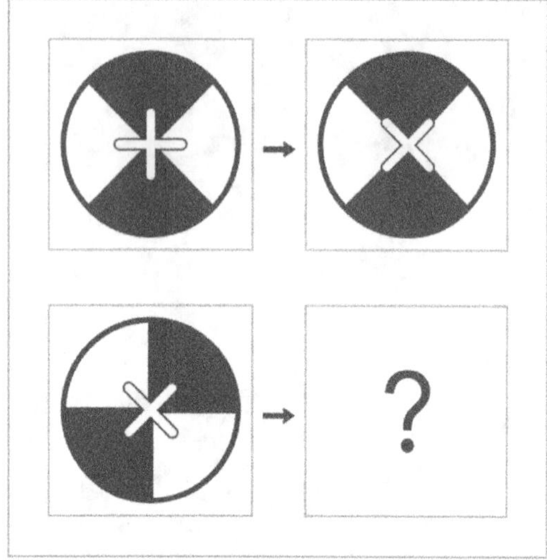

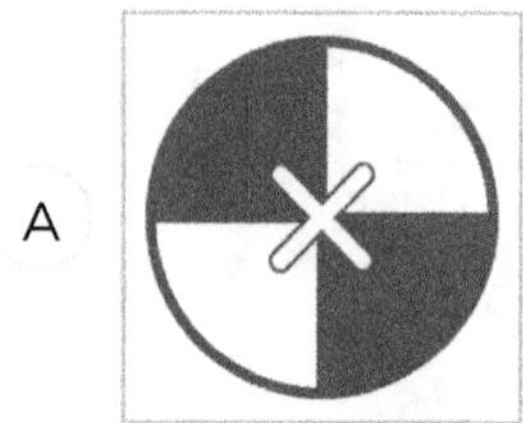 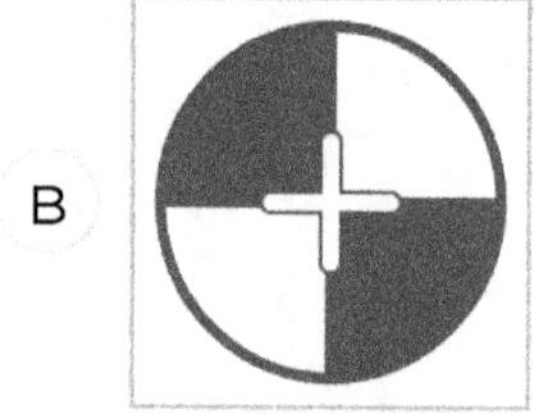

A 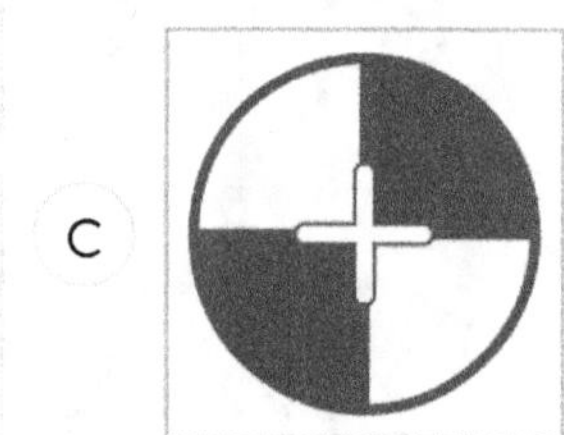

B 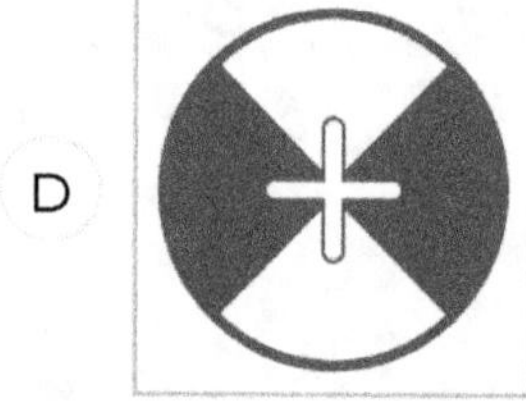

Question 9

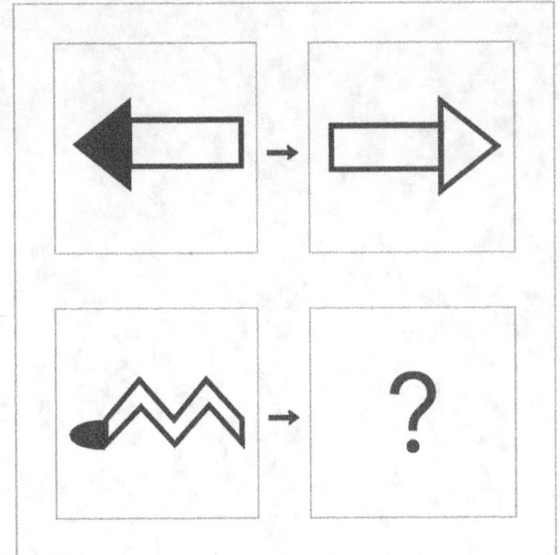

A 

B 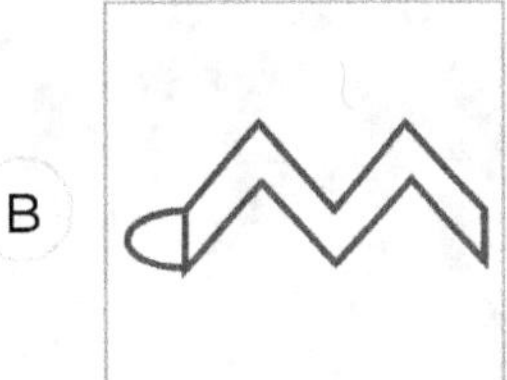

C 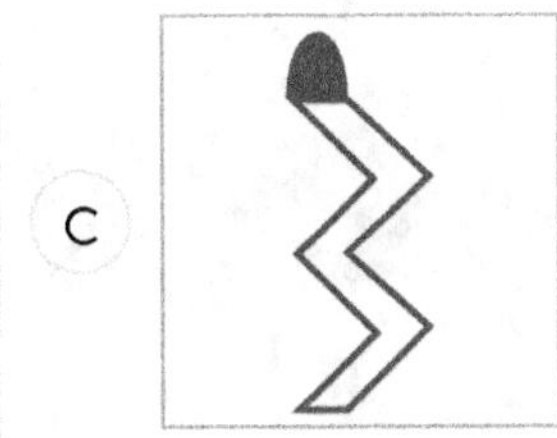

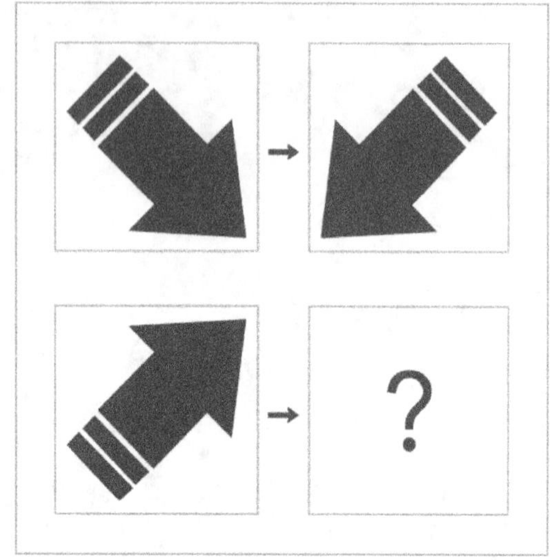

1. a
2. b
3. b
4. d
5. b
6. b
7. a
8. c
9. a
10. C

Non Verbal
Paper Folding

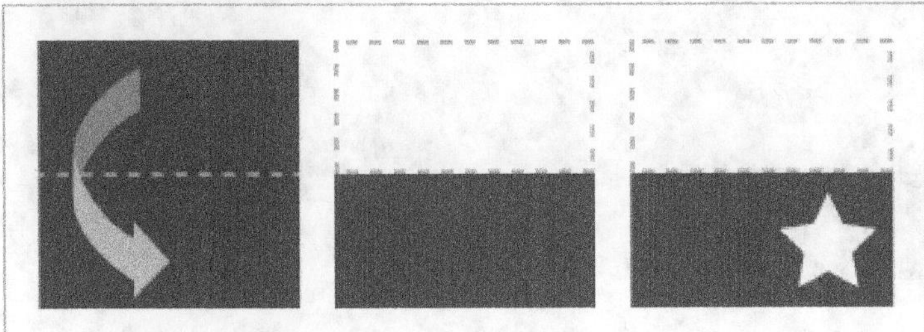

A 

B 

C 

D 

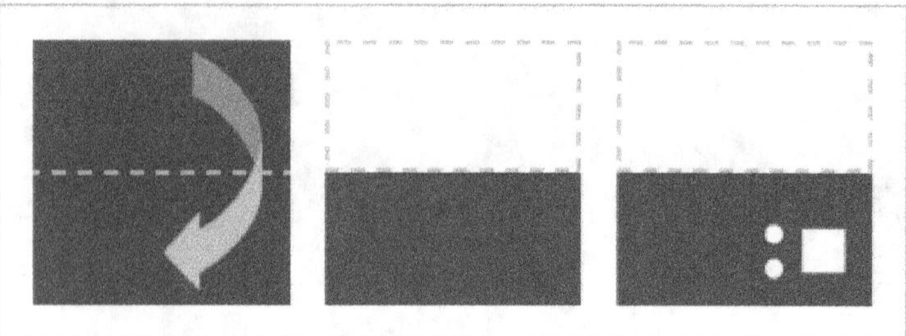

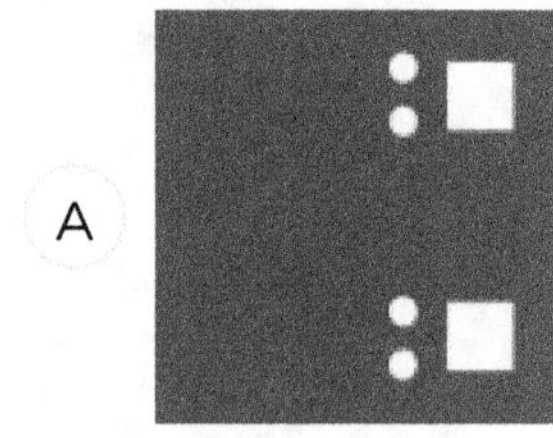

A

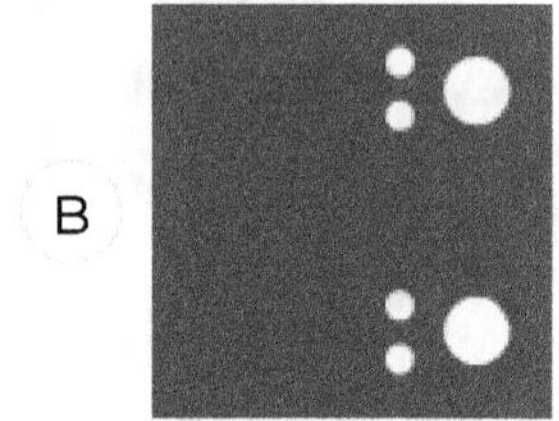

B

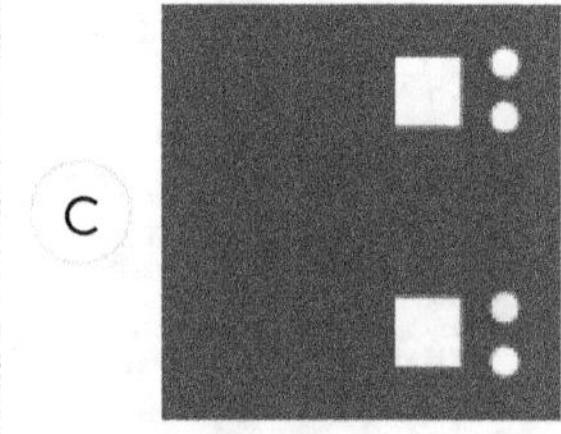

C

D

Question 3

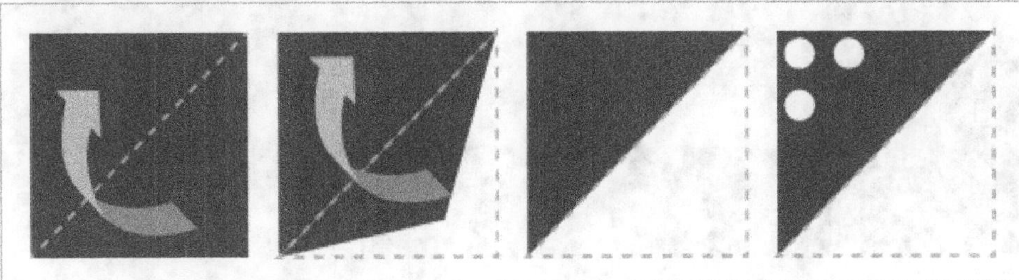

A 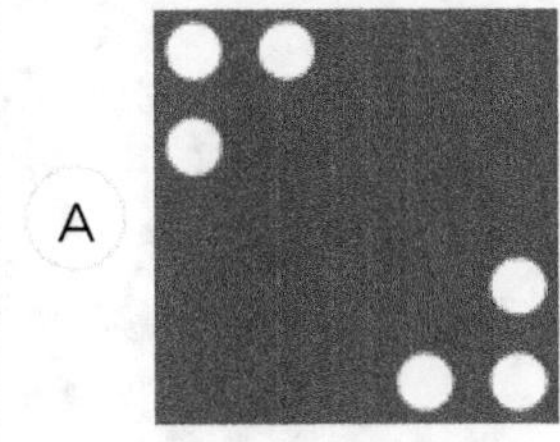

B 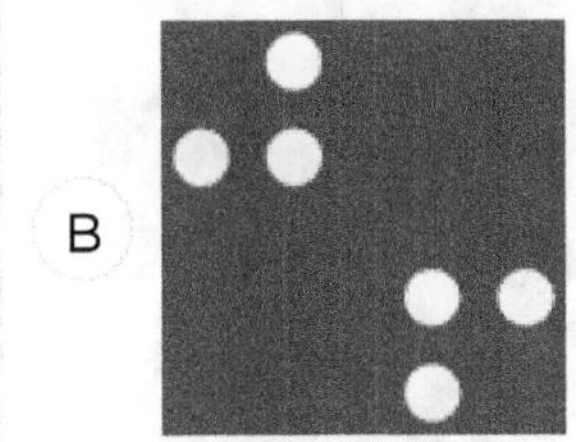

C 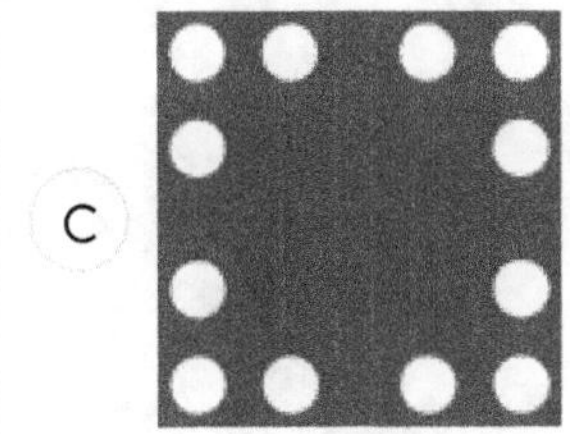

D 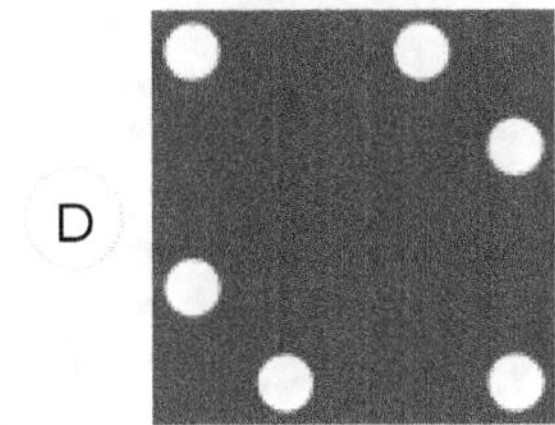

Question 4

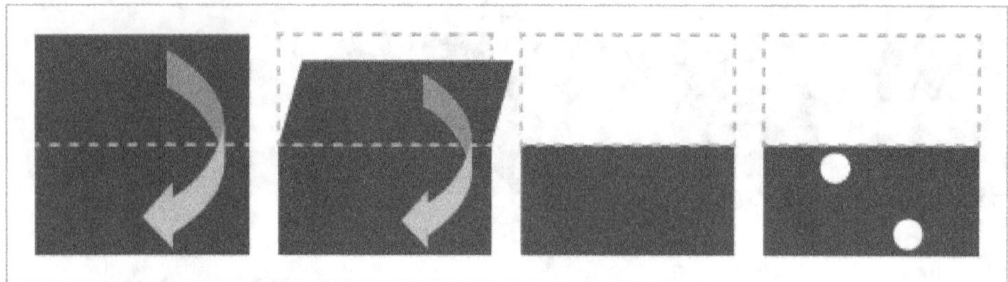

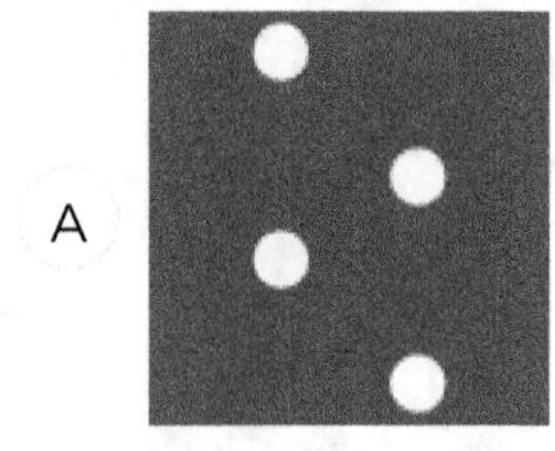

A

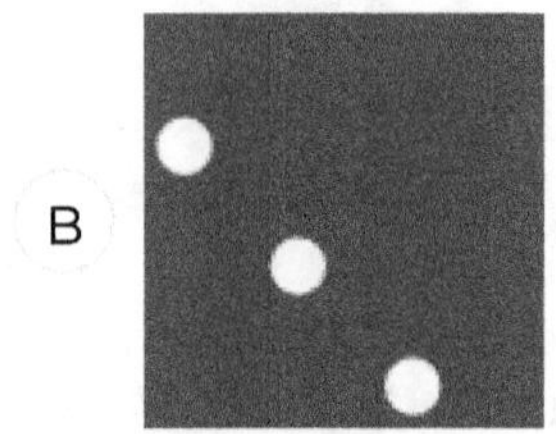

B

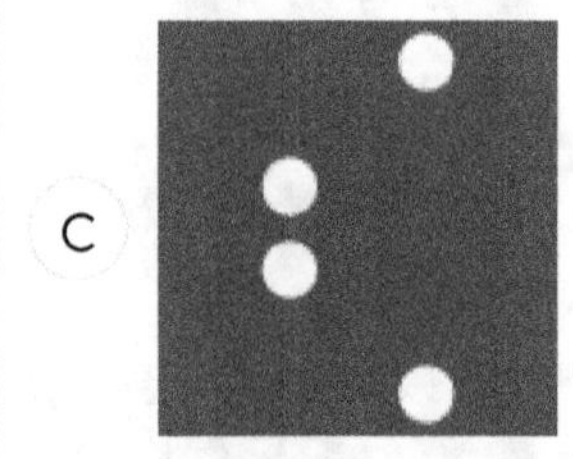

C

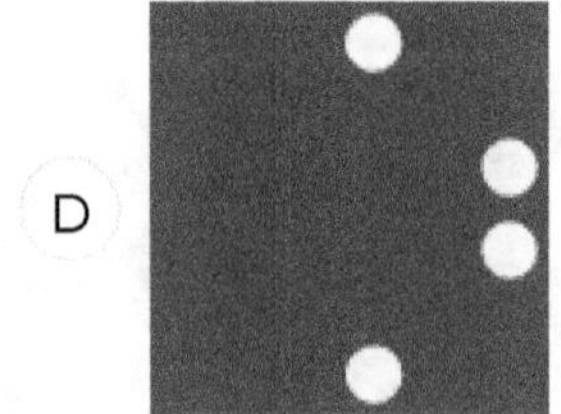

D

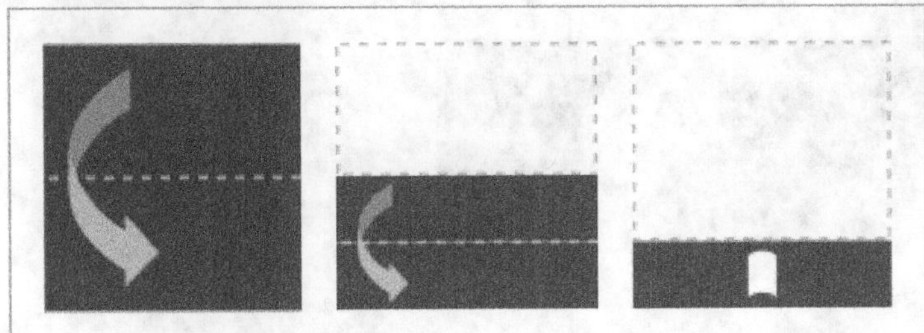

A
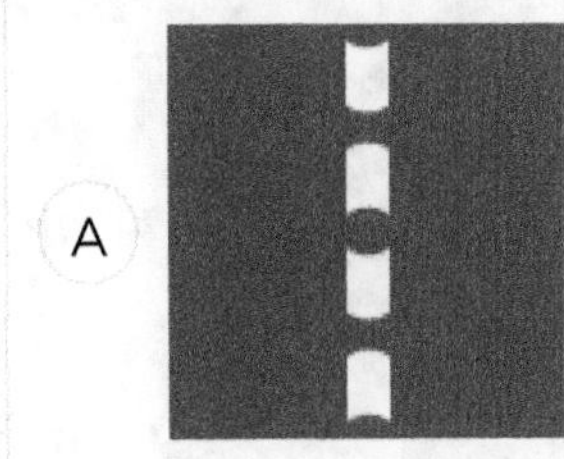

B
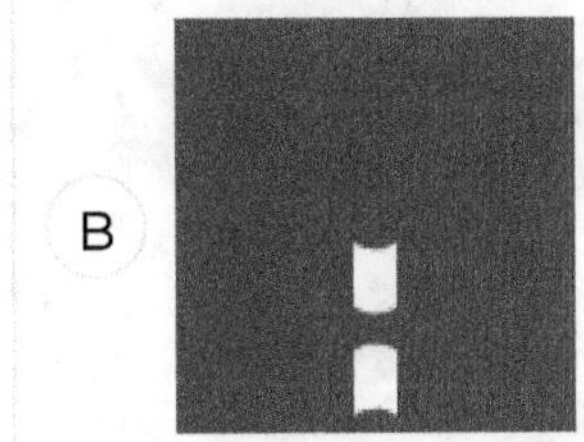

C
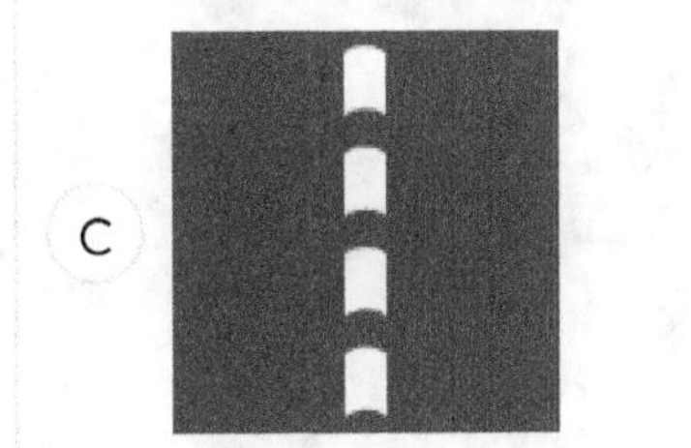

D
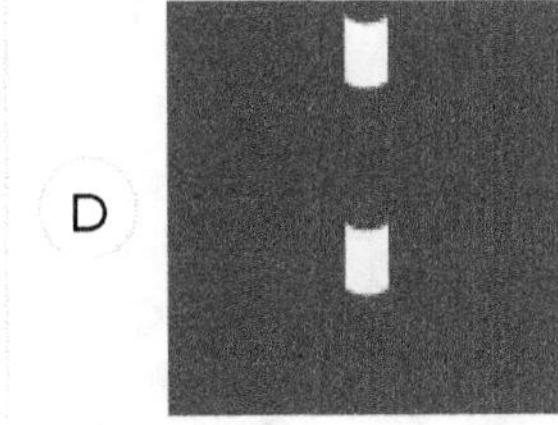

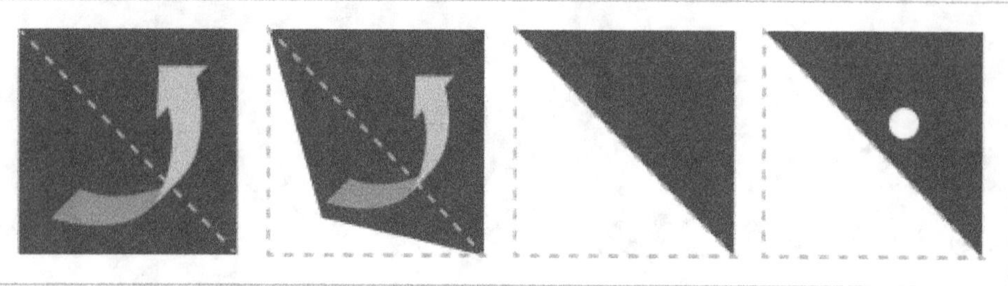

A 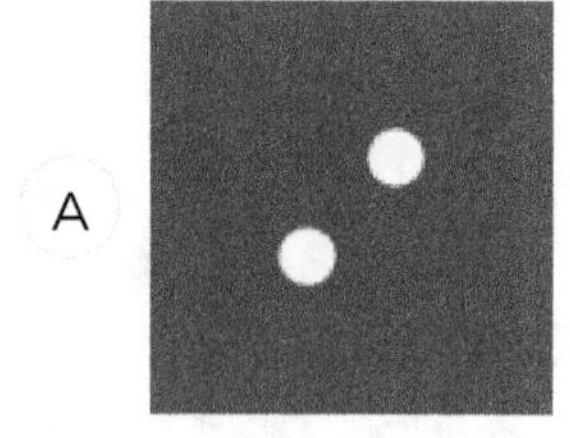

B 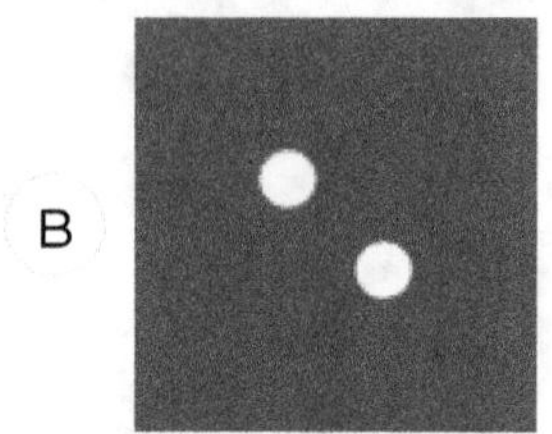

C 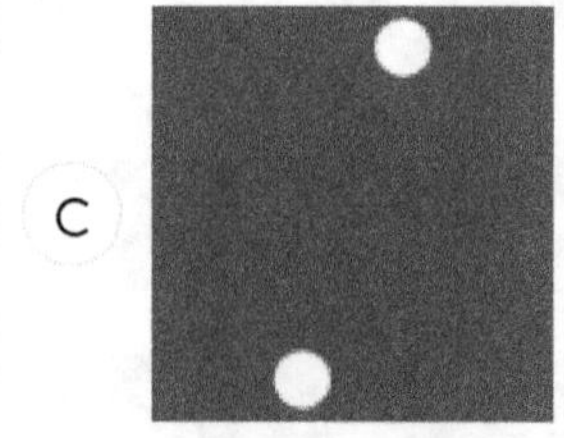

D 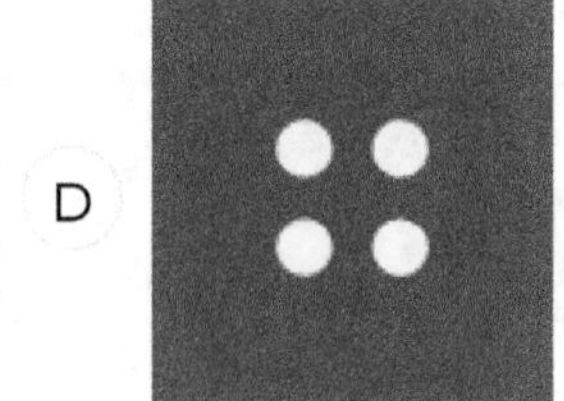

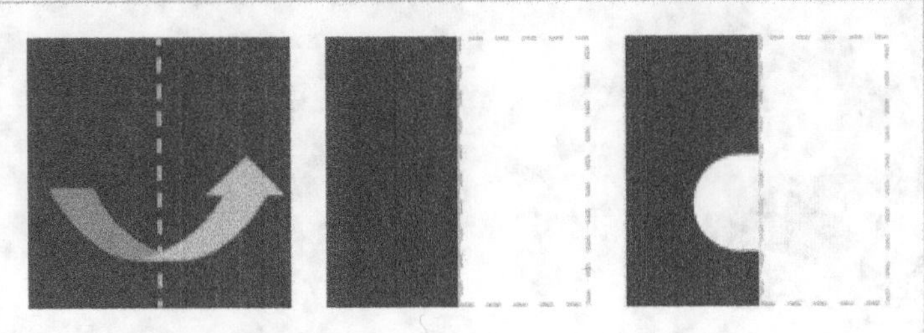

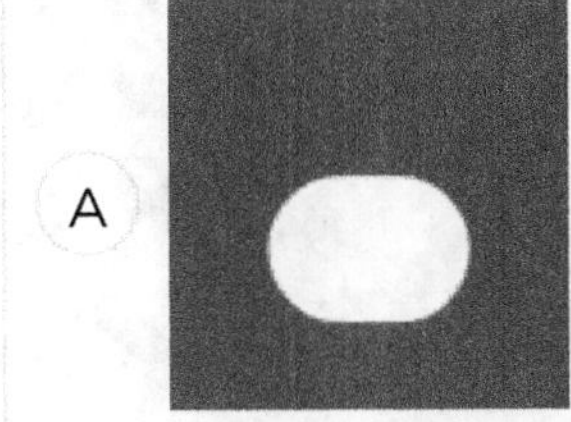

A

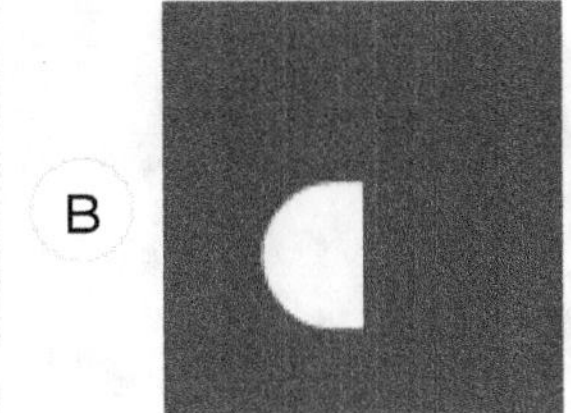

B

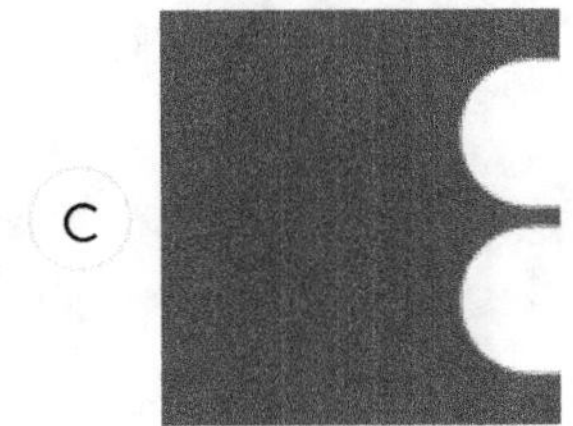

C

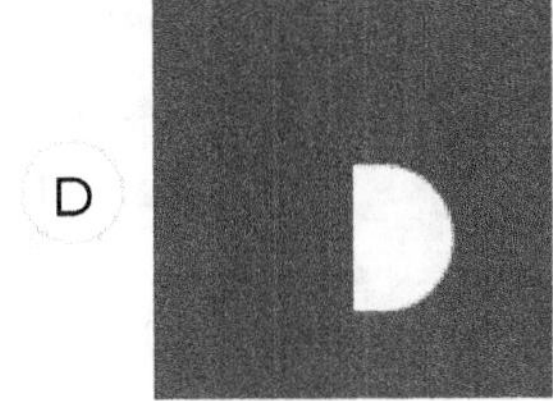

D

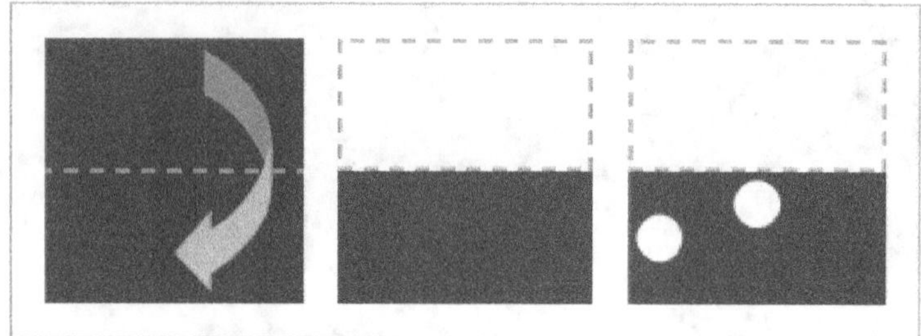

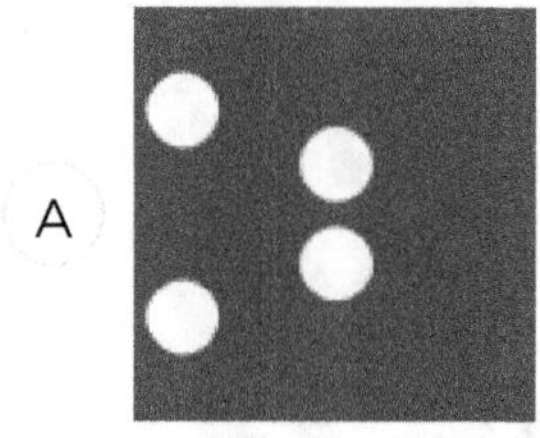

A

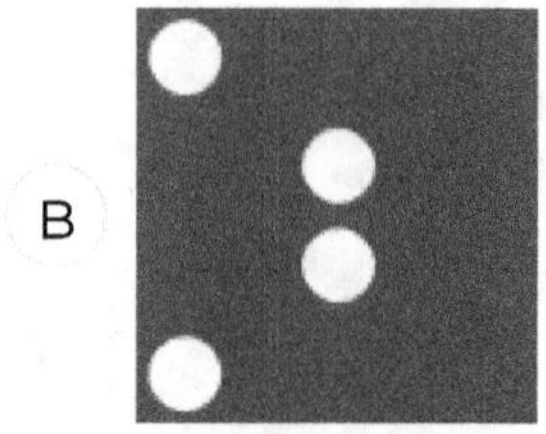

B

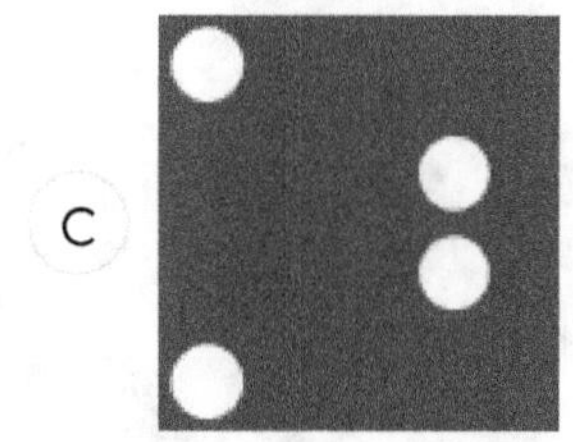

C

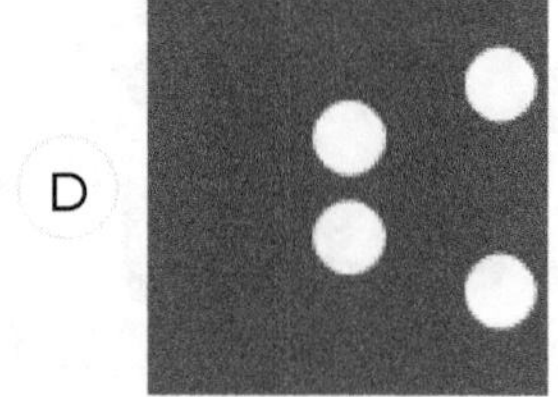

D

Question 9

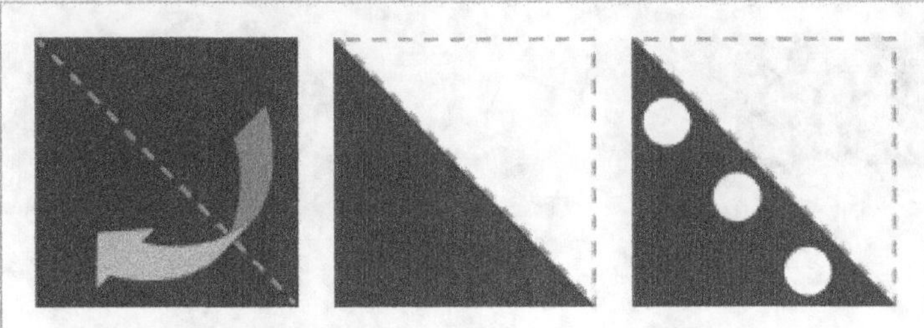

A 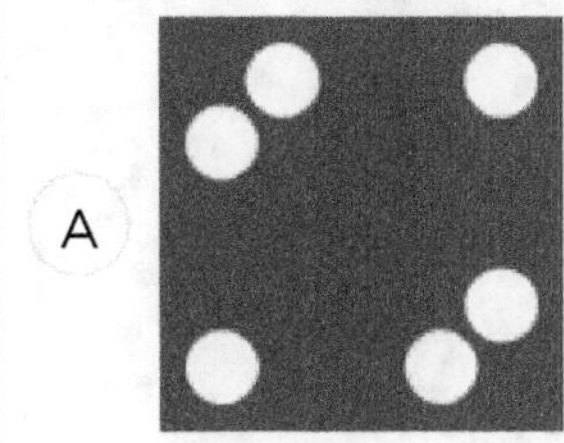

B 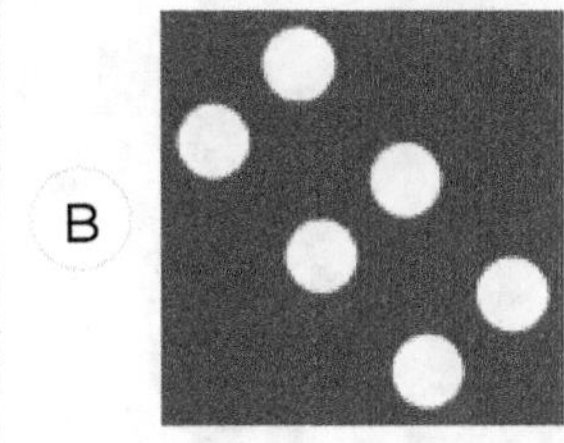

C 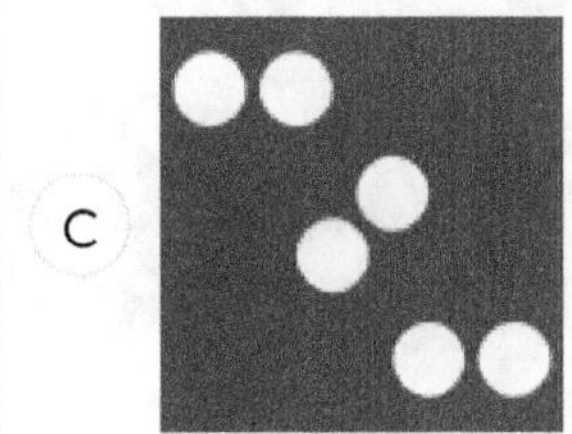

D 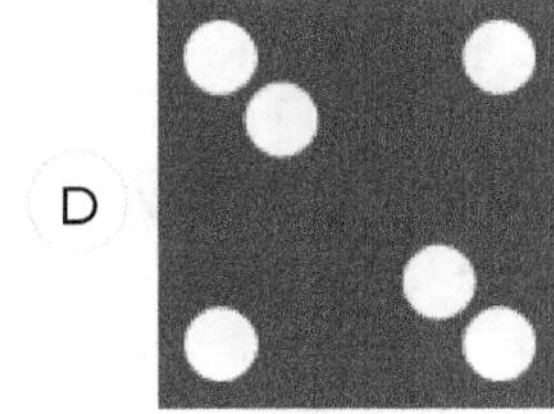

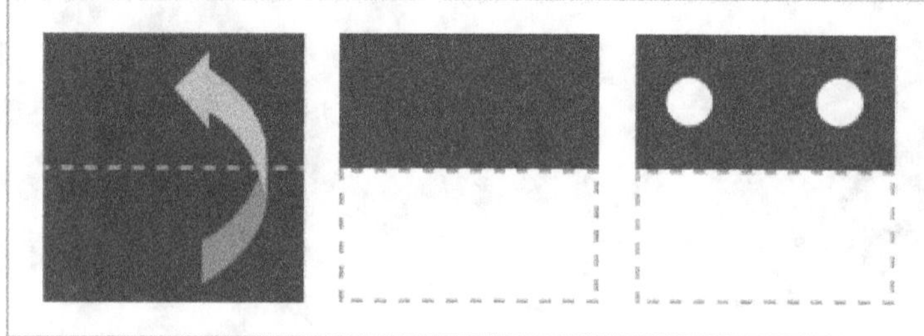

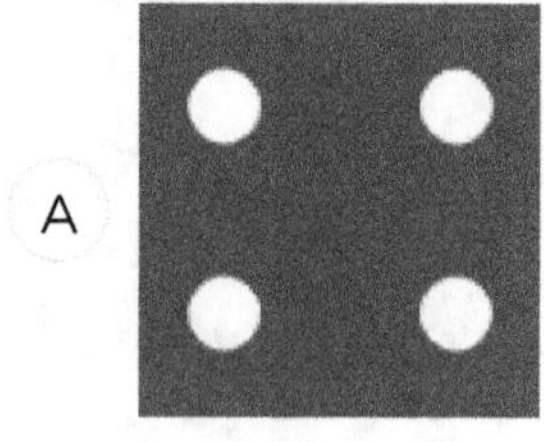

A

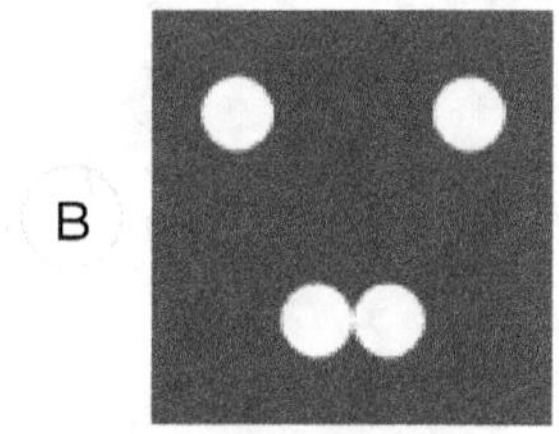

B

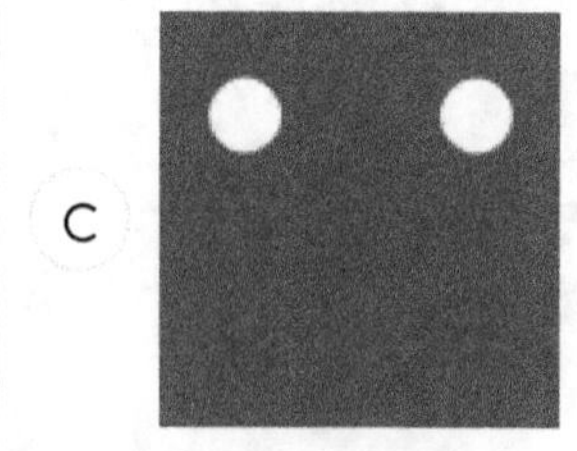

C

D

1. c
2. a
3. a
4. c
5. a
6. a
7. a
8. a
9. b
10. a

Quantitative
Number Analogies

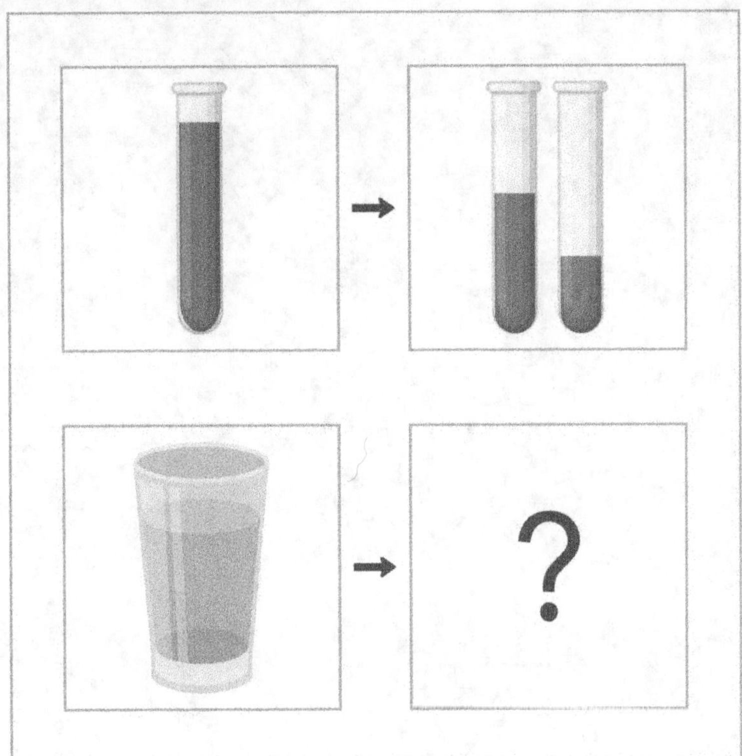

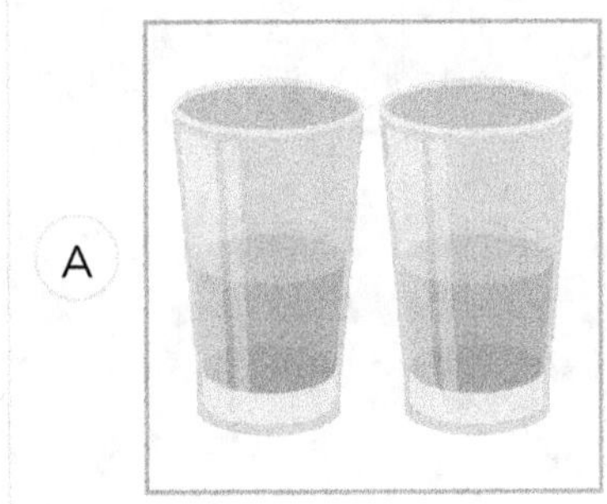

A

B

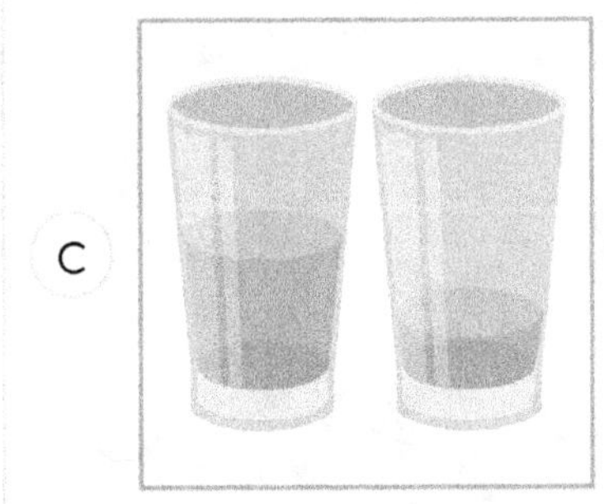

C

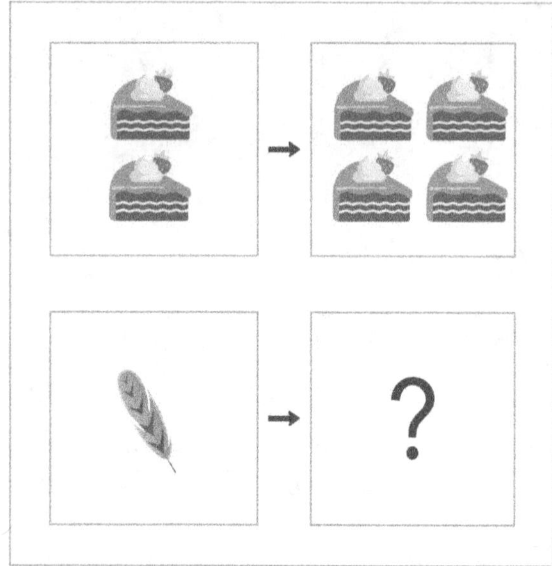

A   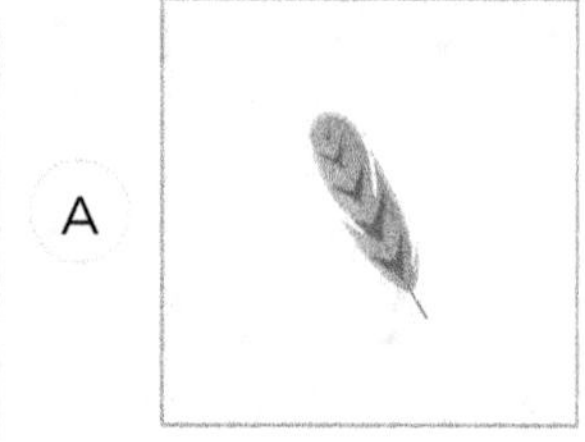

B   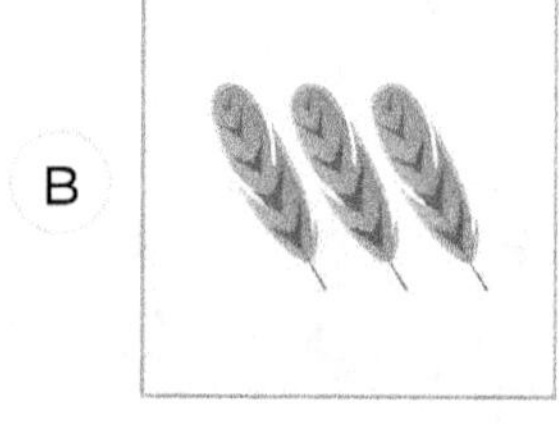

C   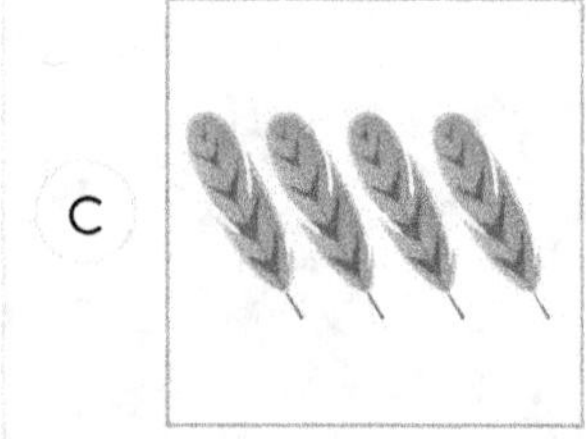

D   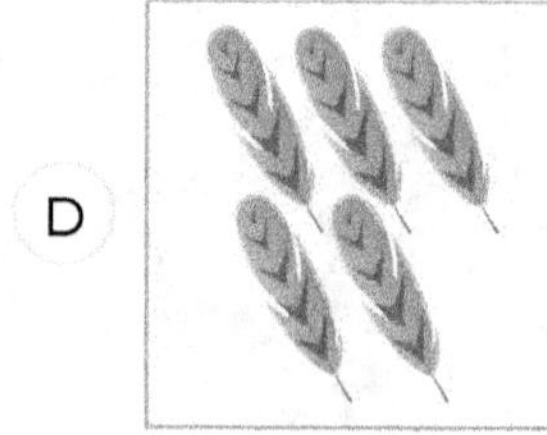

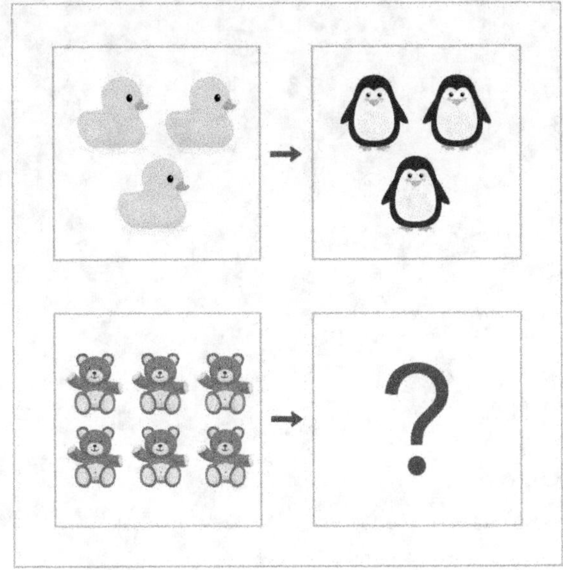

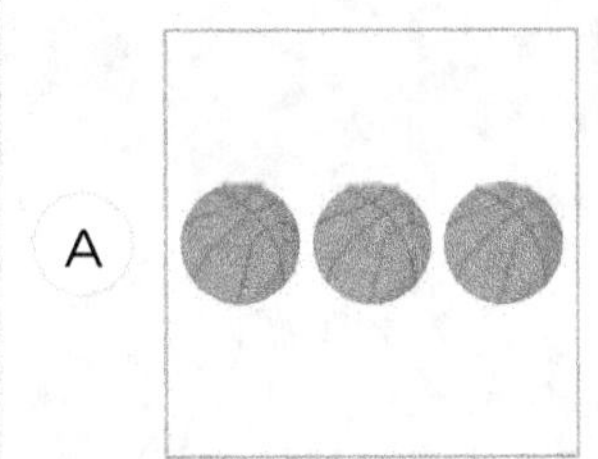

A

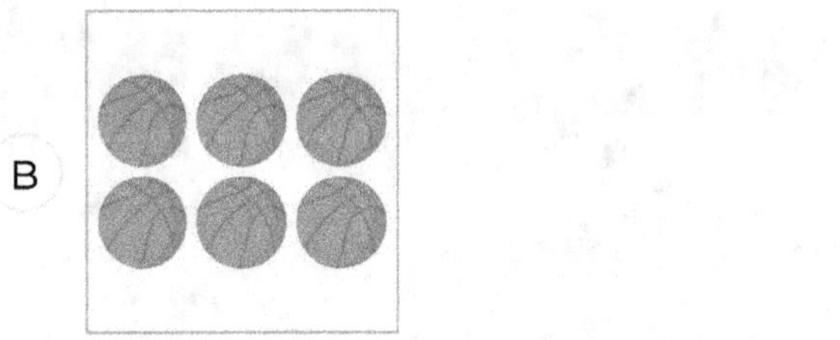

B

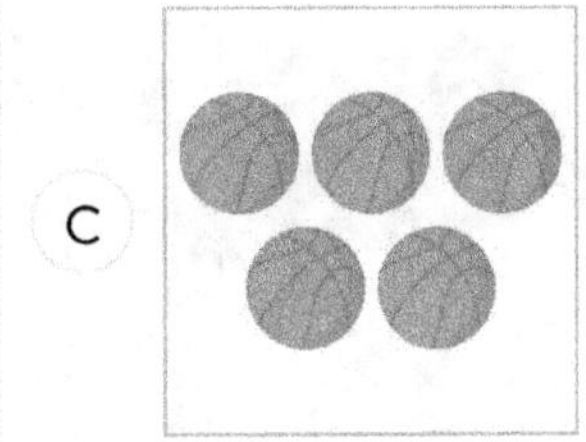

C

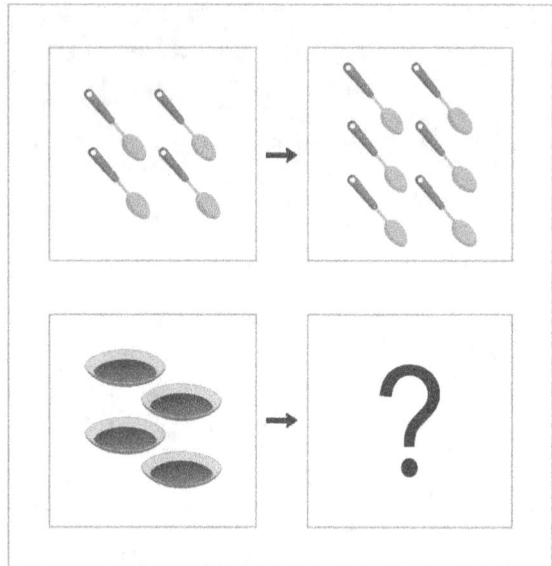

A 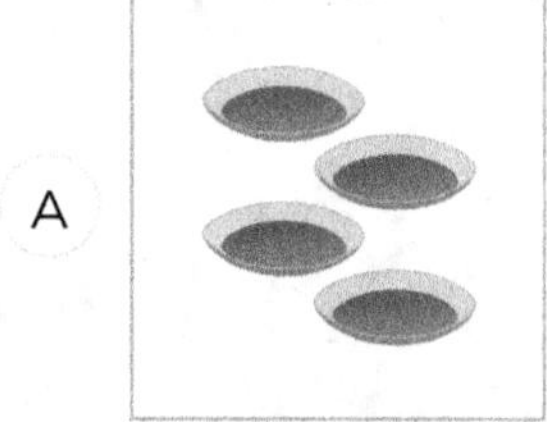

B 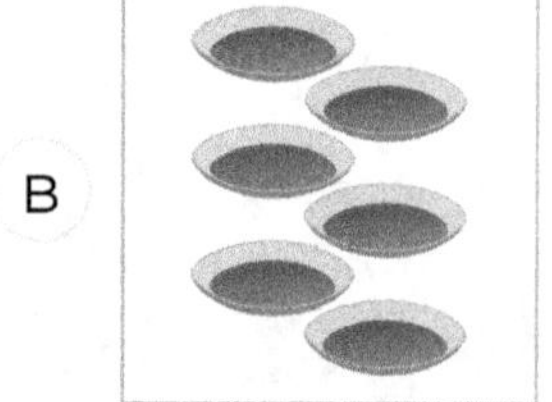

C 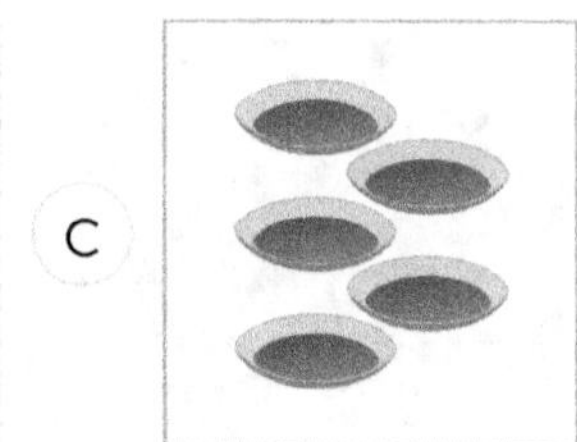

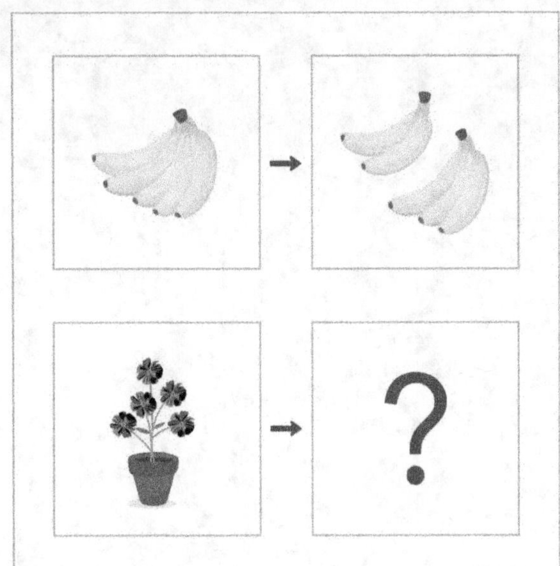

A

B

C

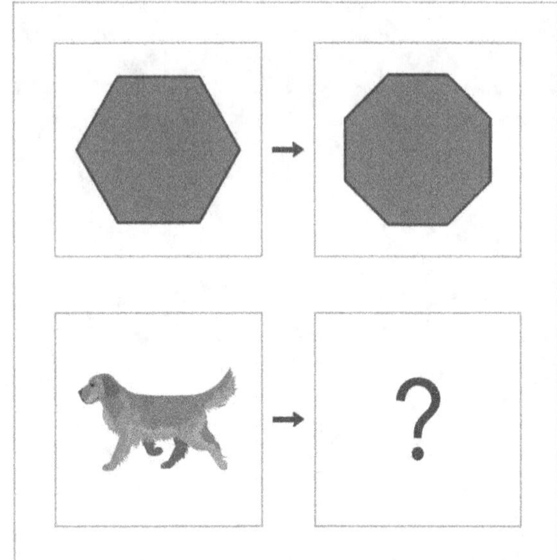

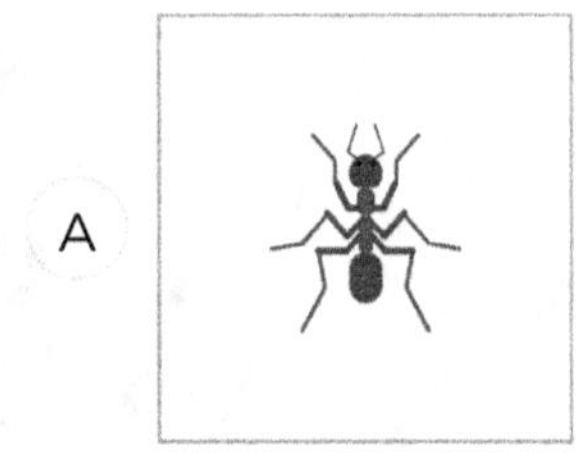 

A 

B 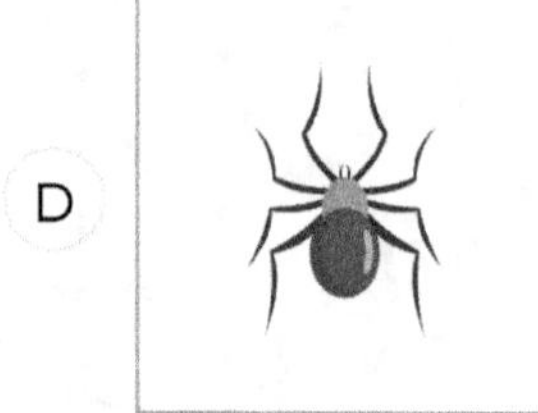

A

B

C

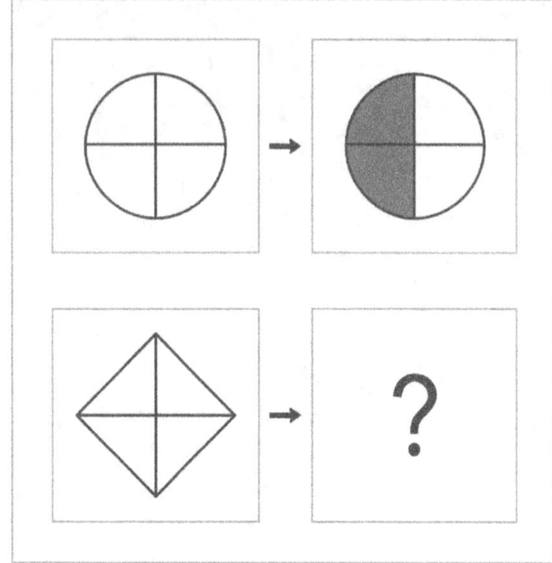

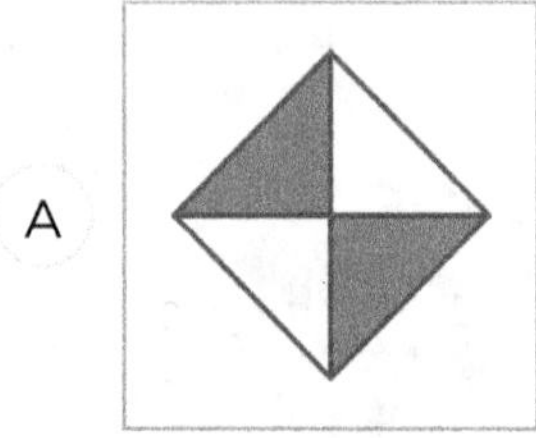

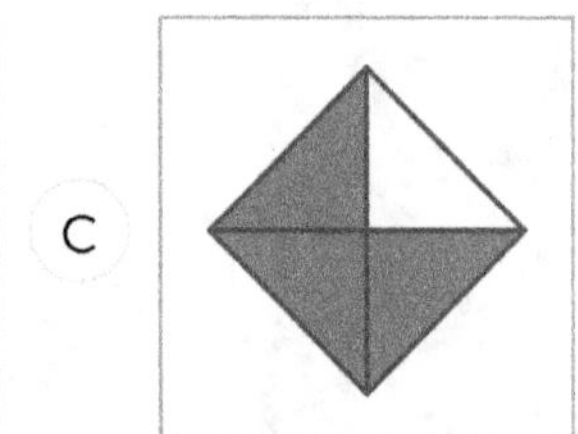

A 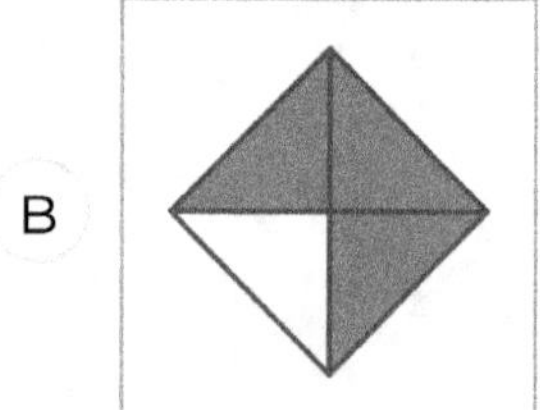

B 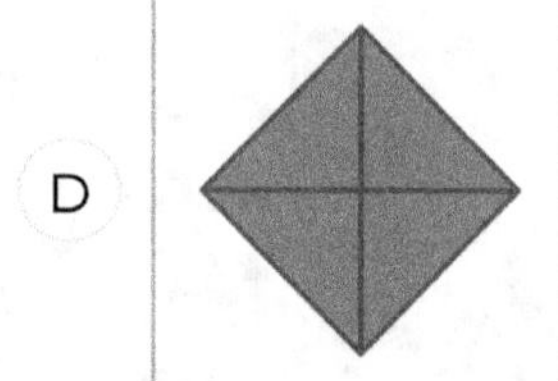

C

D

Quantitative

Number Analogies

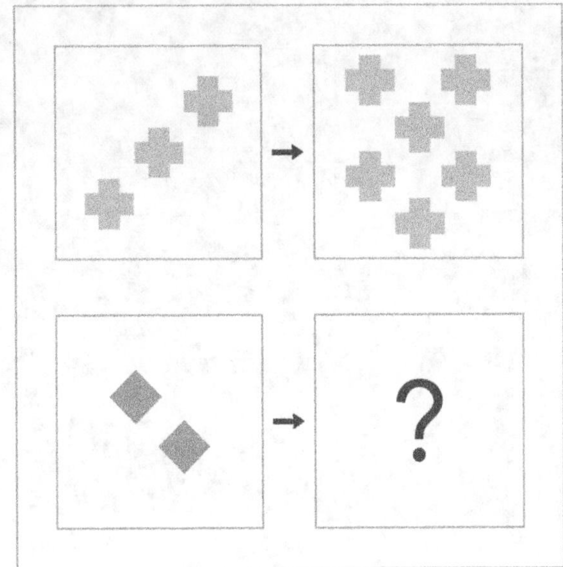

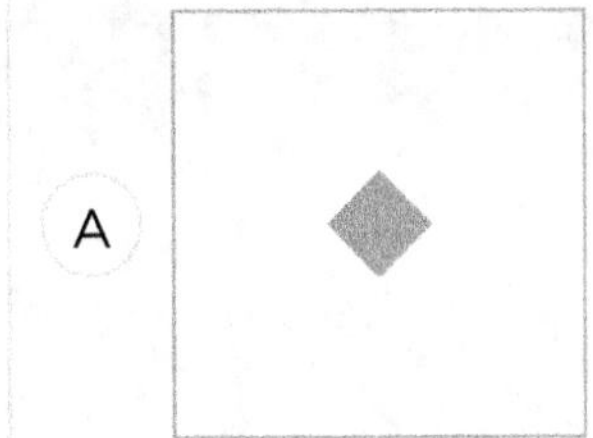

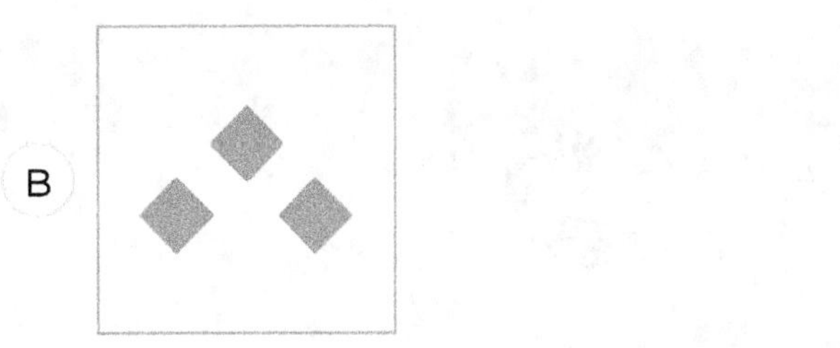

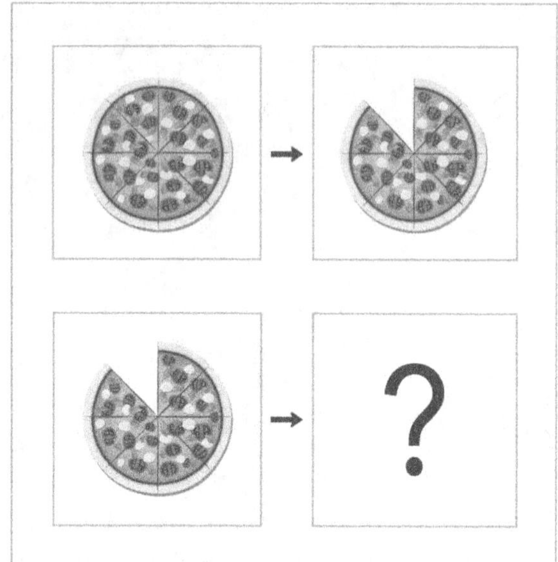

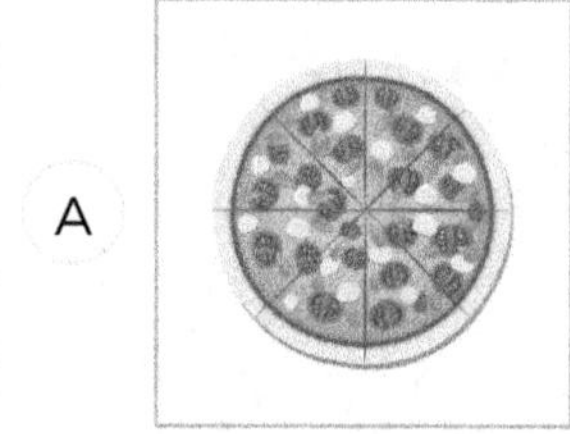

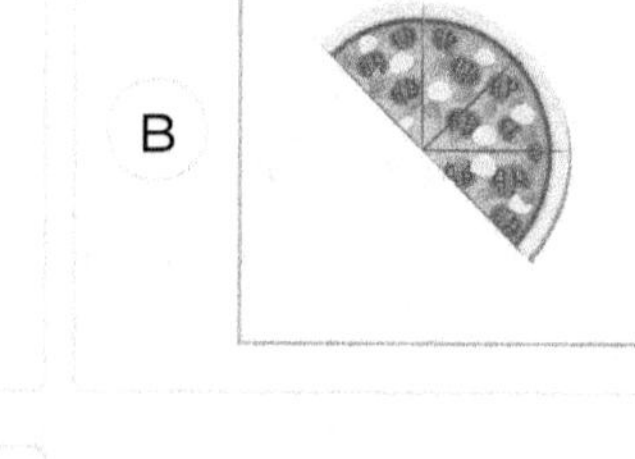

A

B

C

1. c
2. b
3. b
4. b
5. b
6. a
7. b
8. a
9. c
10. c

Quantitative
Number Puzzles

Question 1

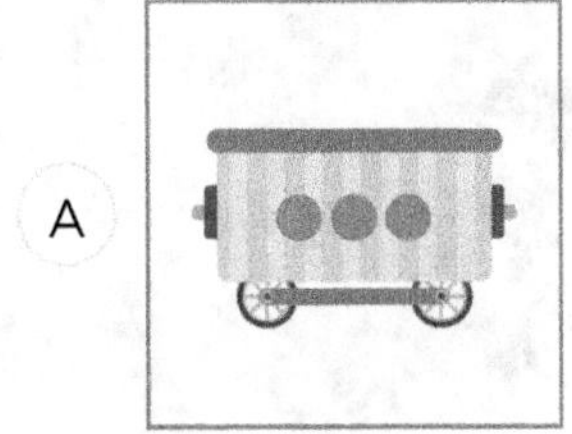
A

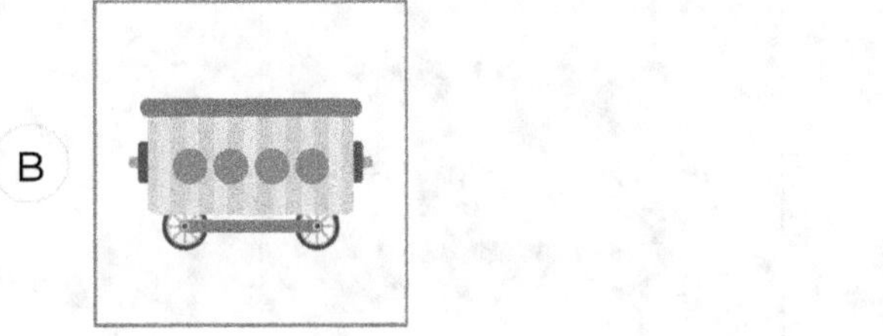
B

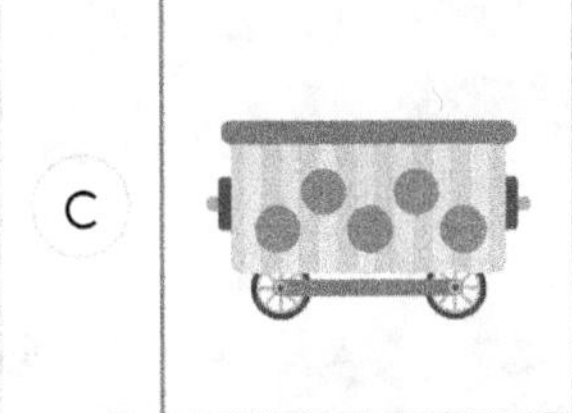
C

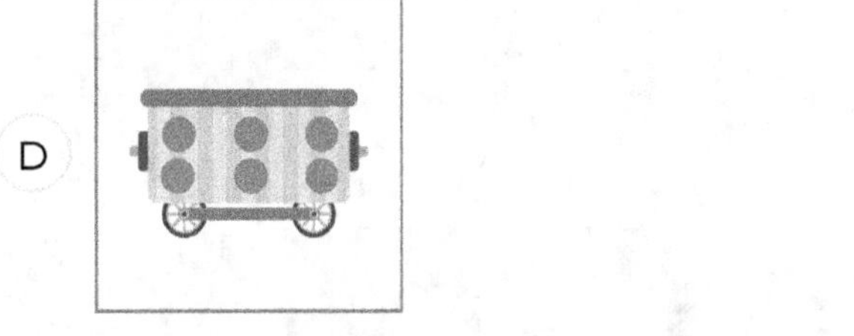
D

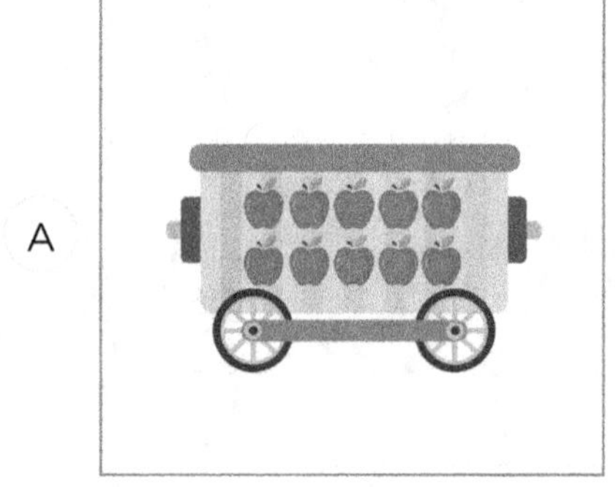

A

B

C

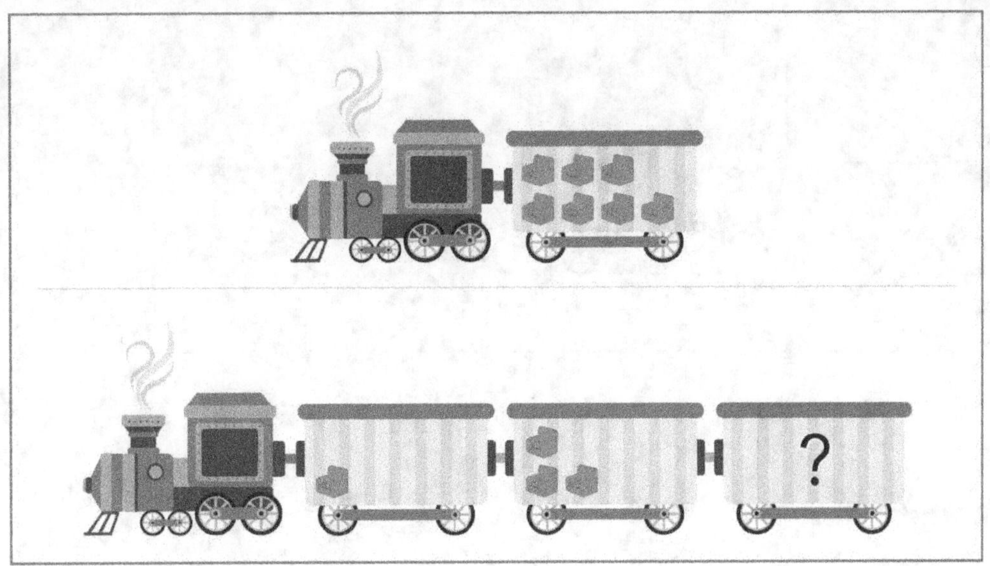

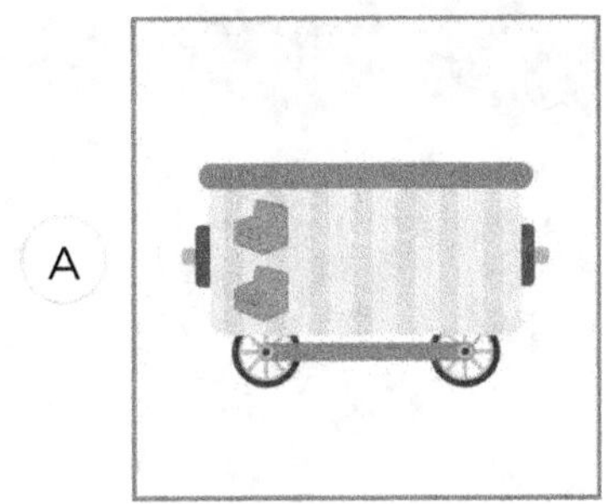

A

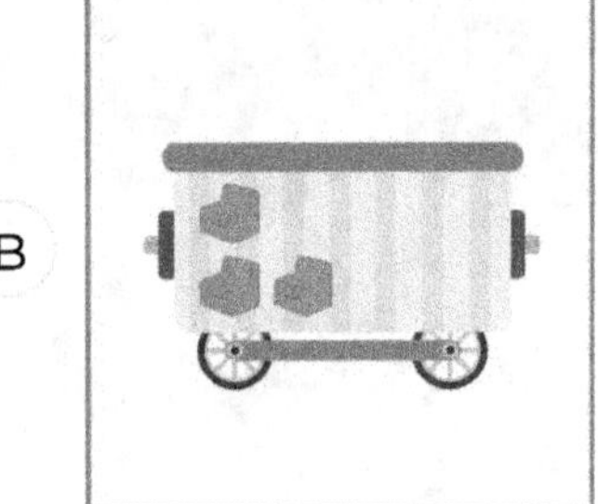

B

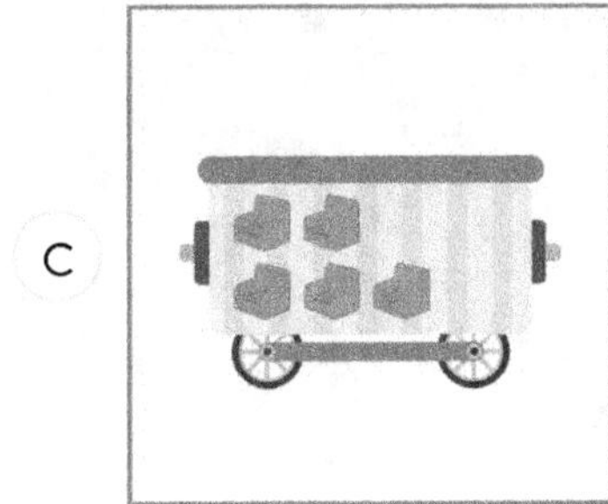

C

A
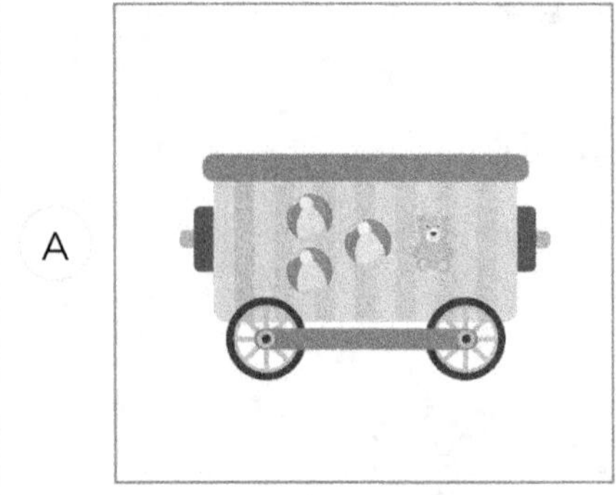

B
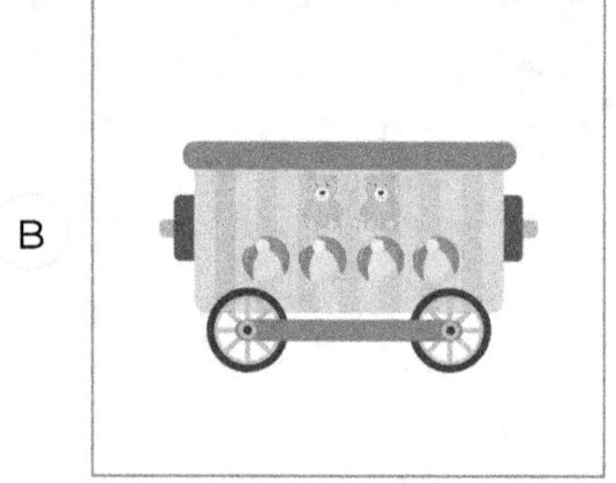

C
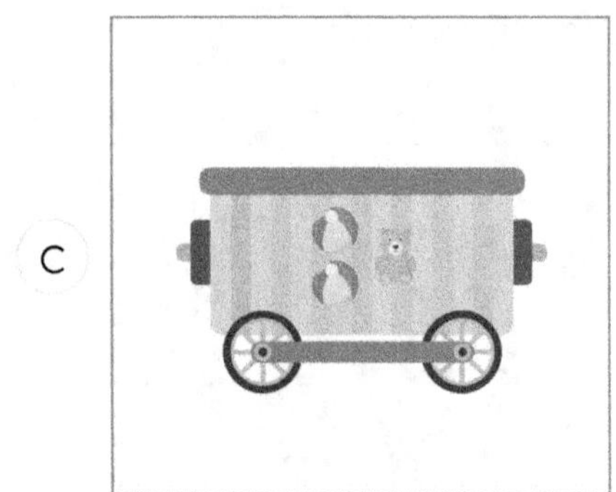

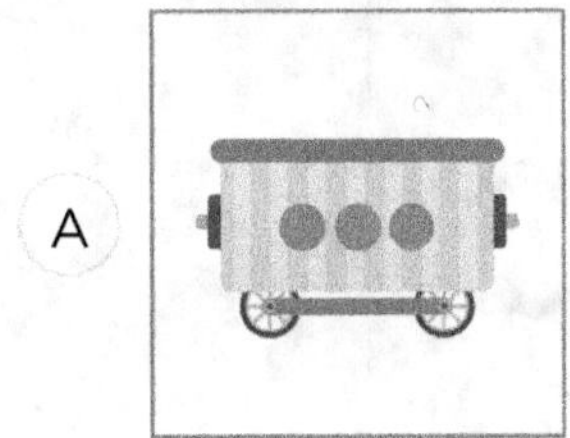

A

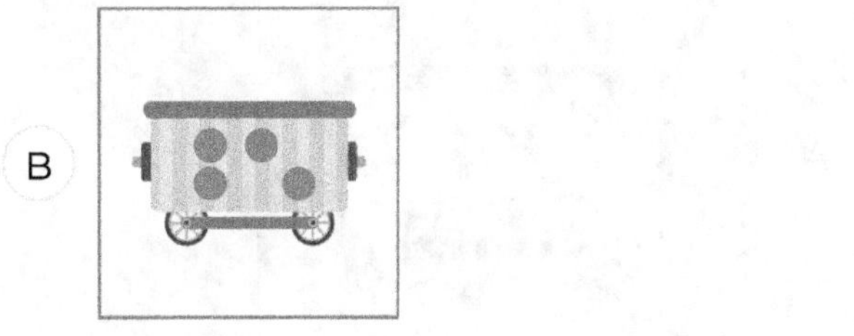

B

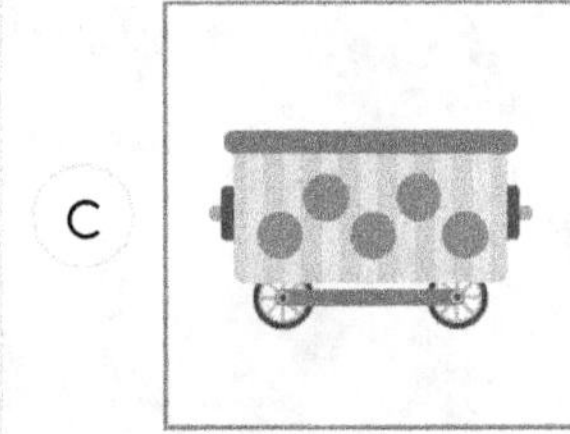

C

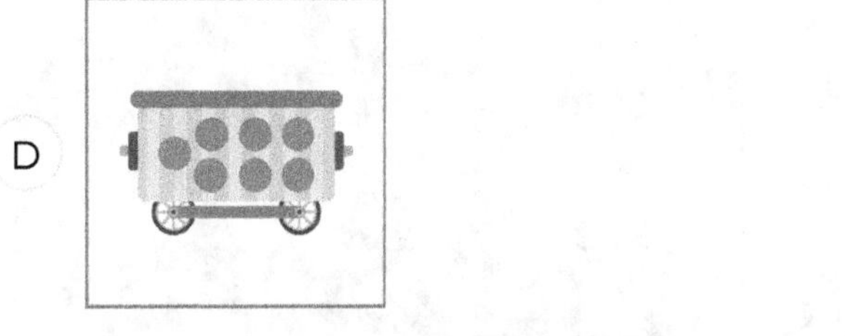

D

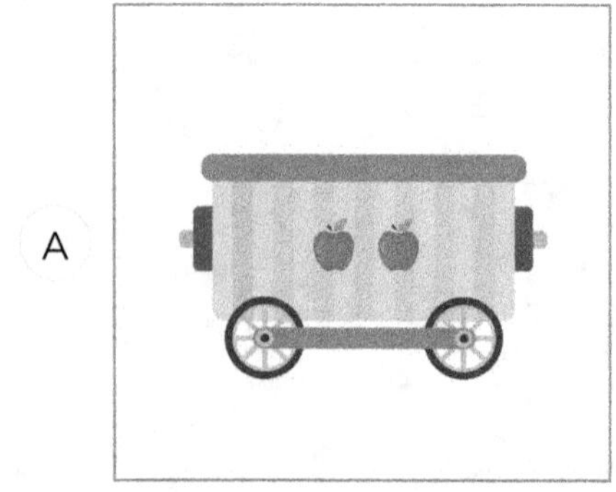

A

B

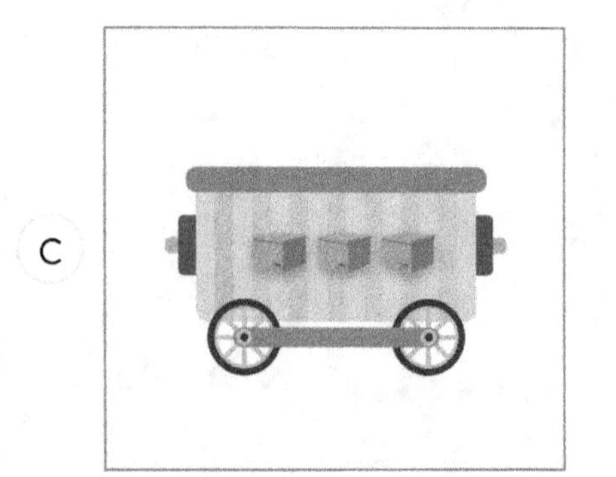

C

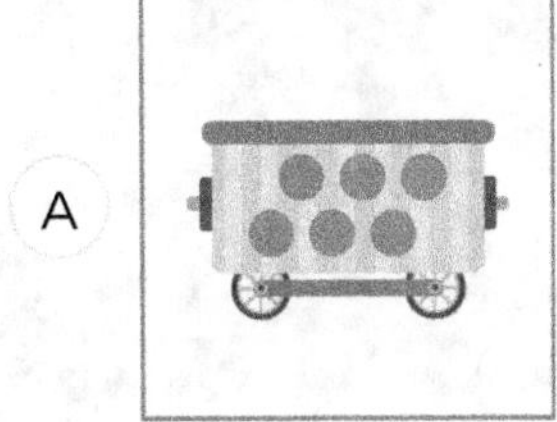

A

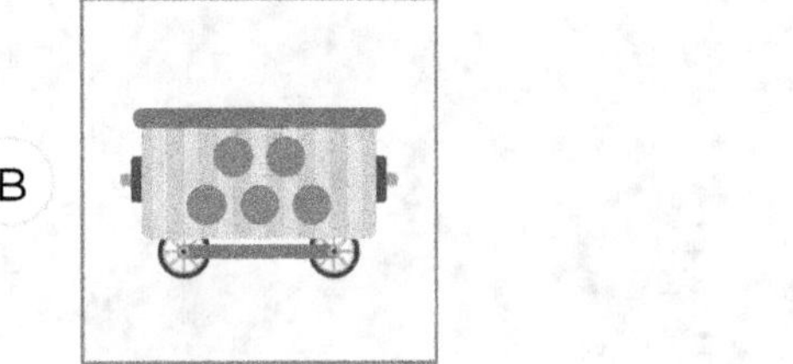

B

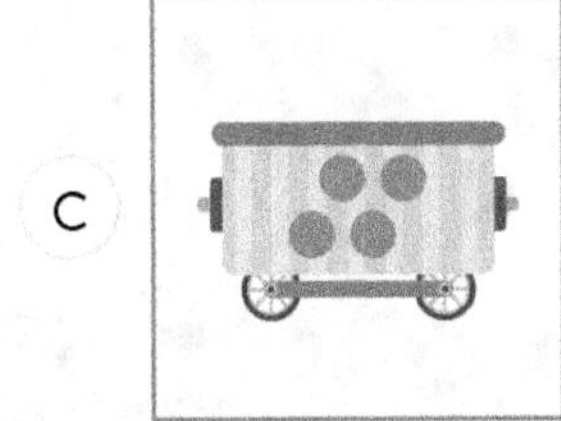

C

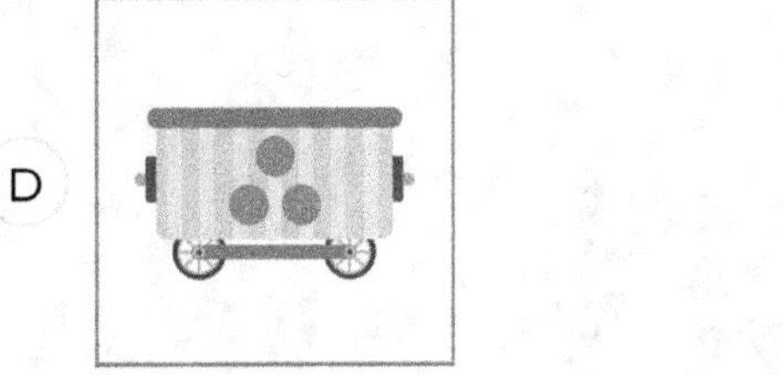

D

Question 8

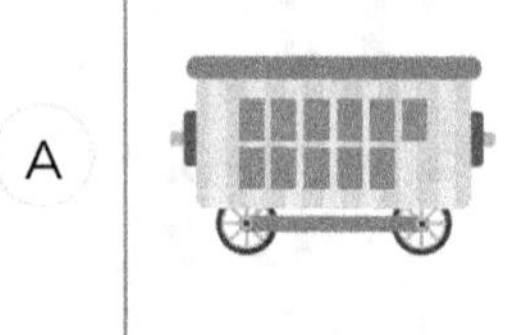

A

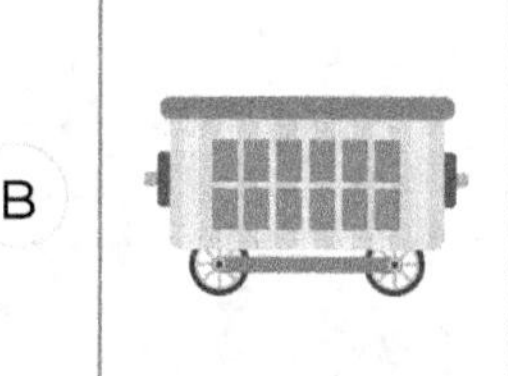

B

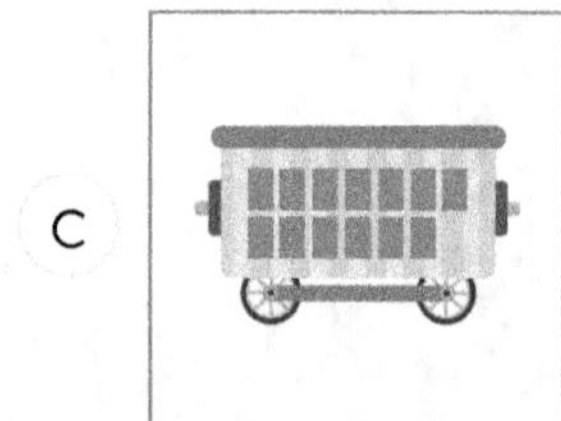

C

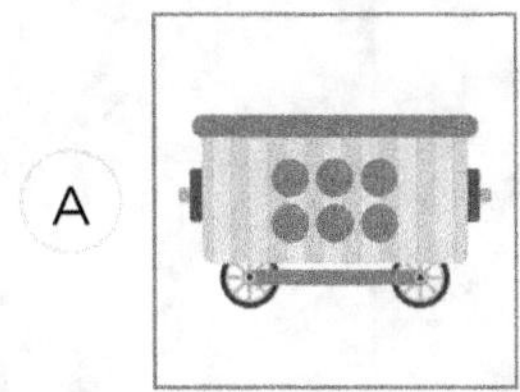

A

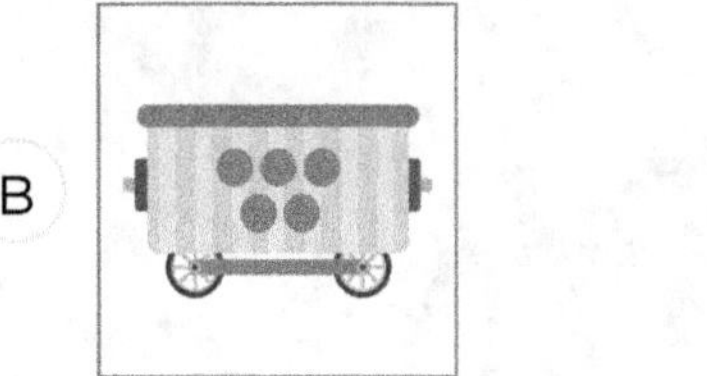

B

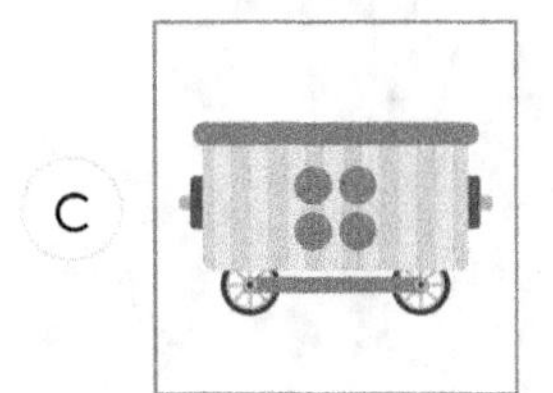

C

A

B

C

1. b
2. c
3. b
4. c
5. d
6. a
7. a
8. a
9. c
10. c

Quantitative
Number Series

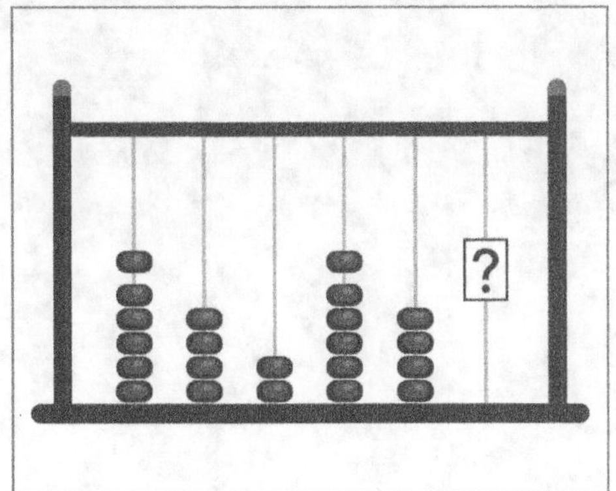

A. 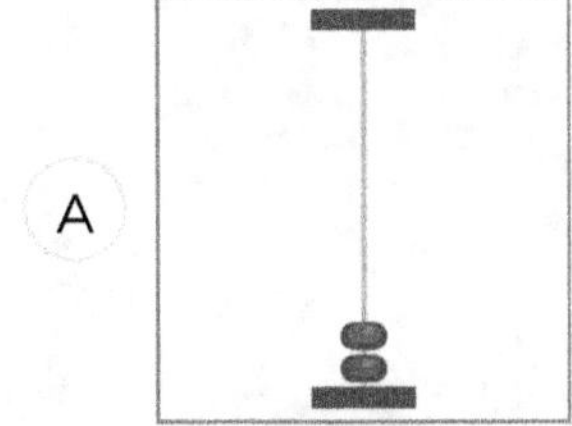

B. 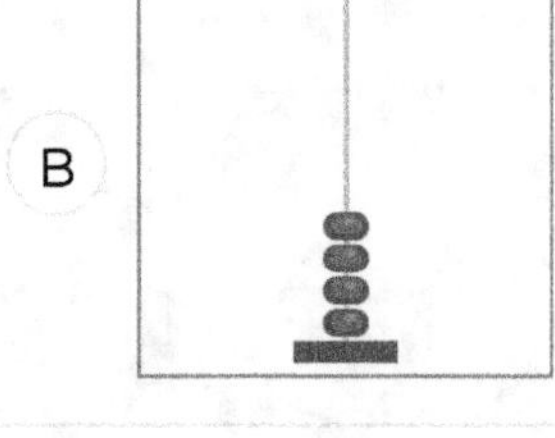

C. 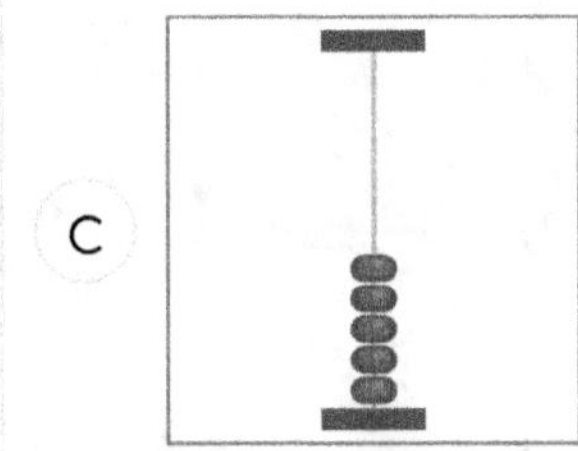

D. 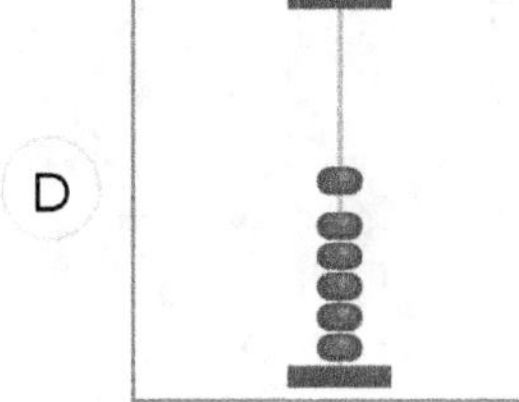

Question 2

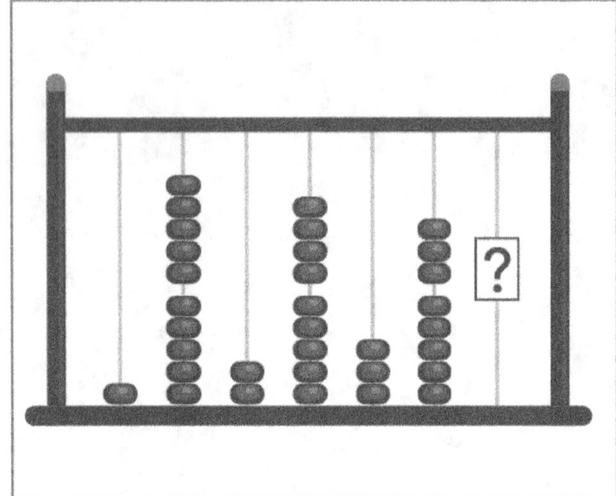

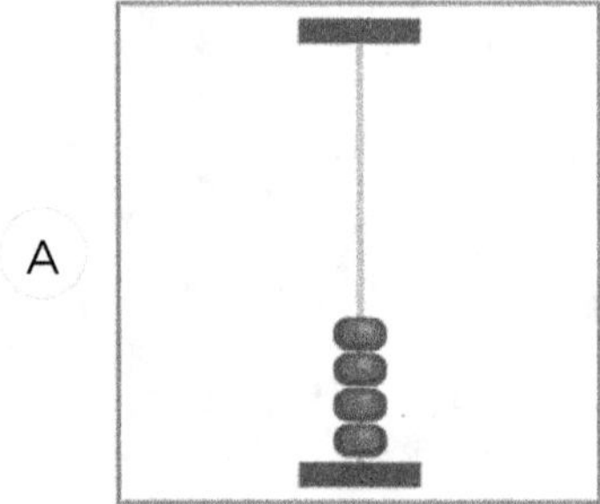

A

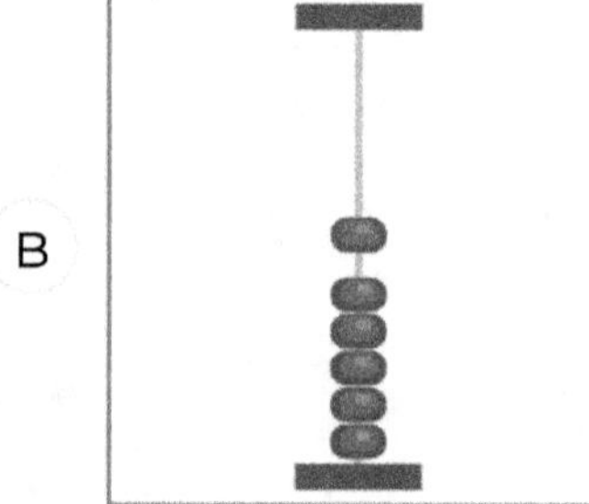

B

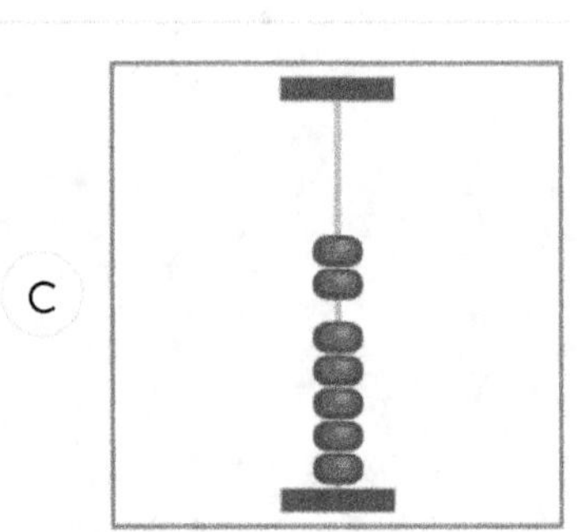

C

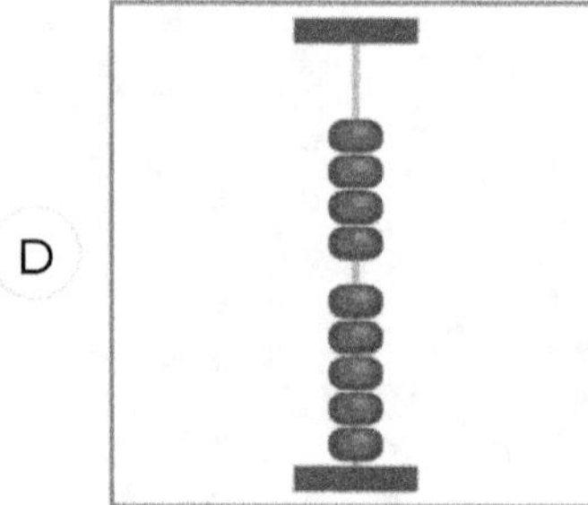

D

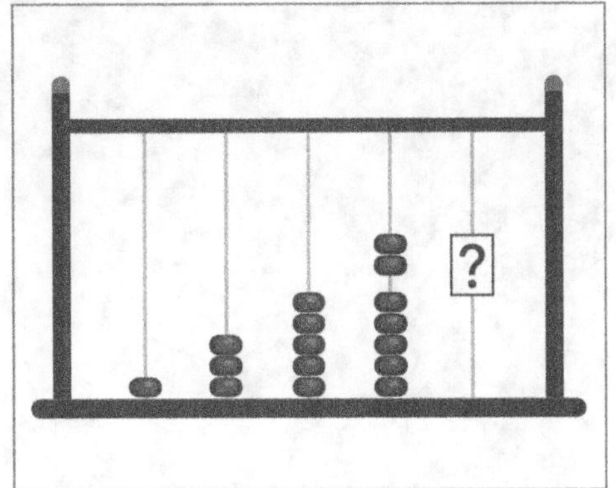

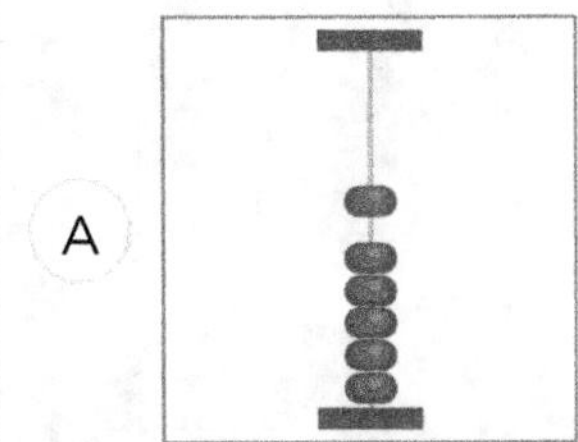

A

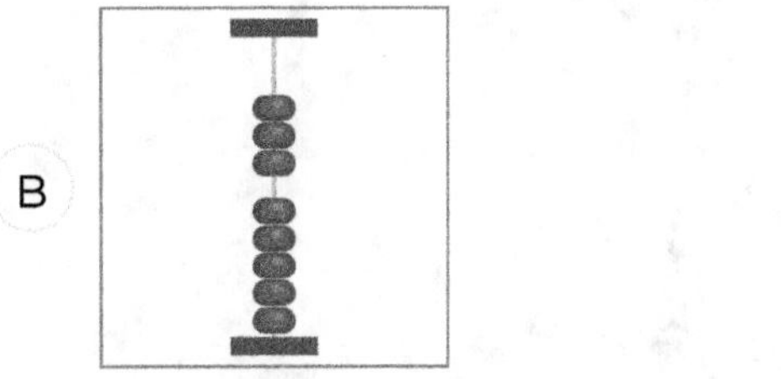

B

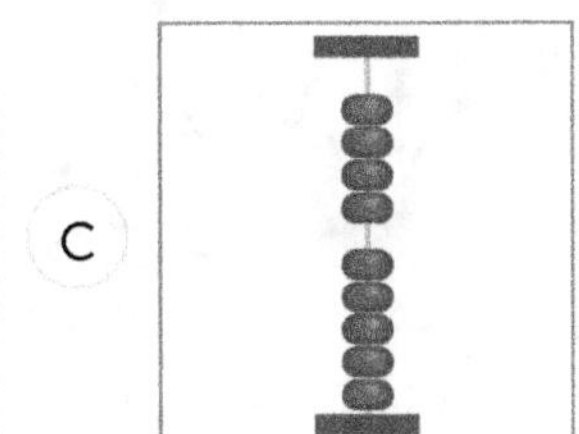

C

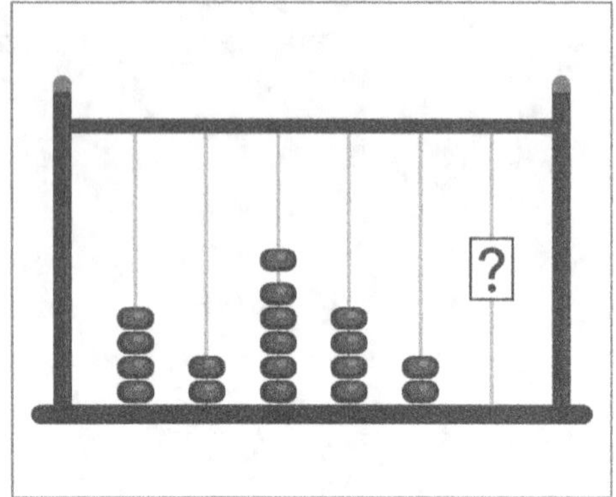

A

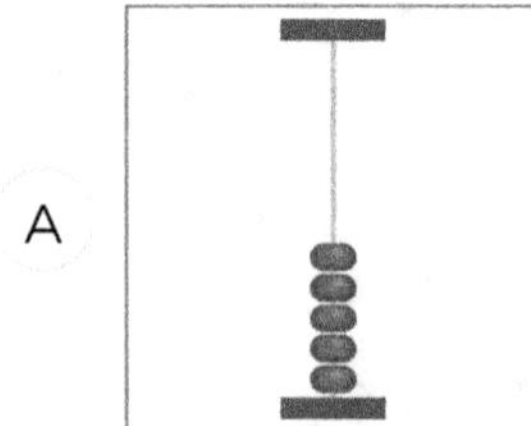

B

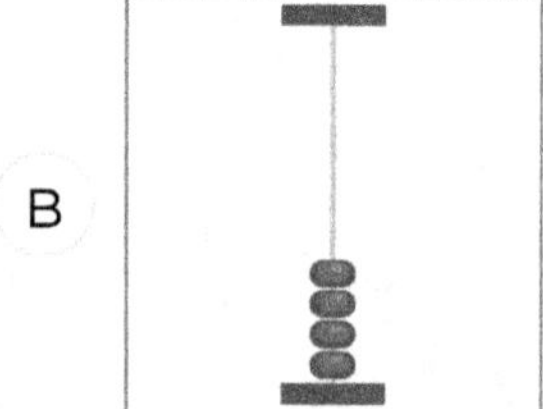

C

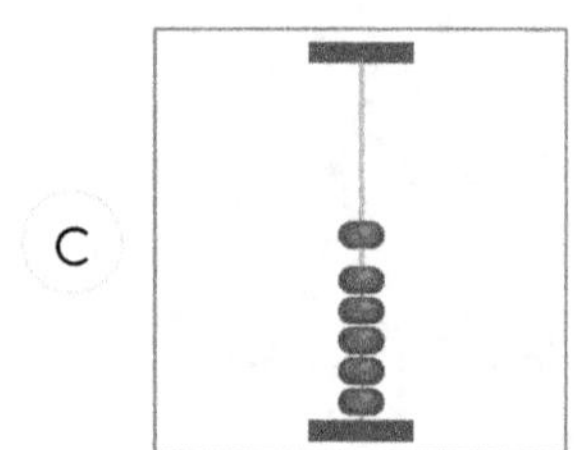

D

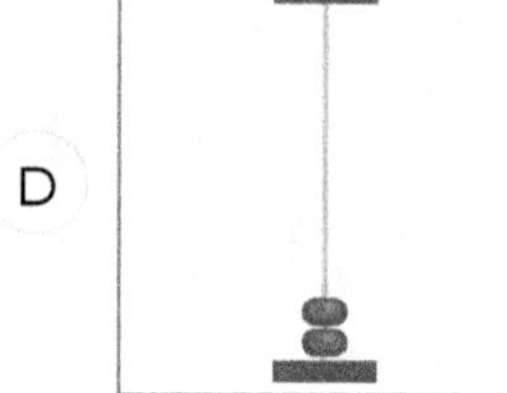

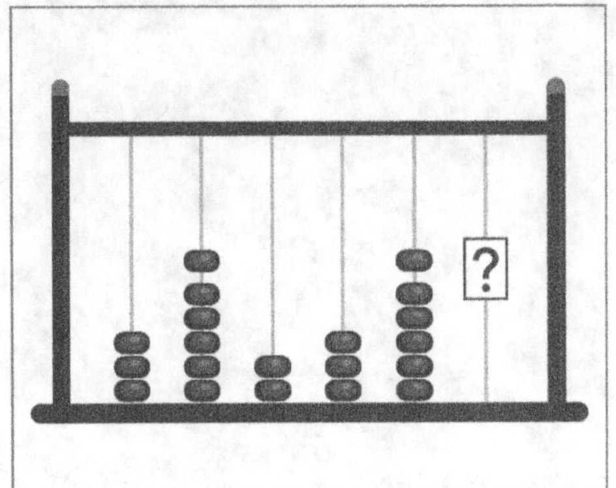

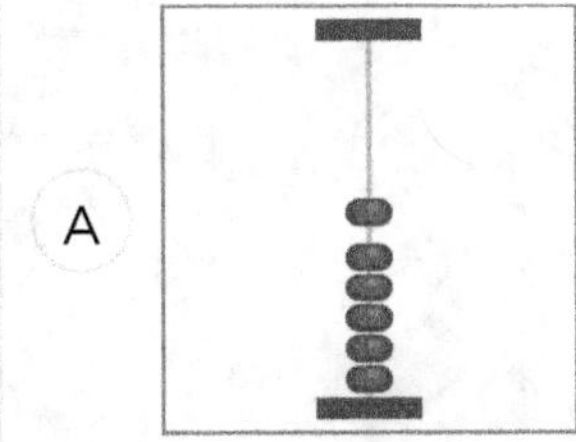

A

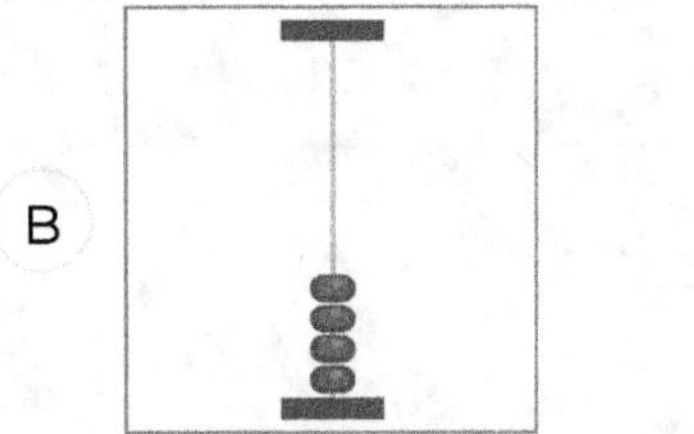

B

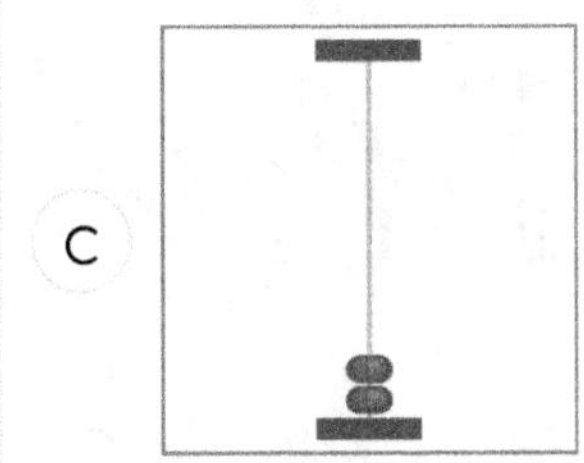

C

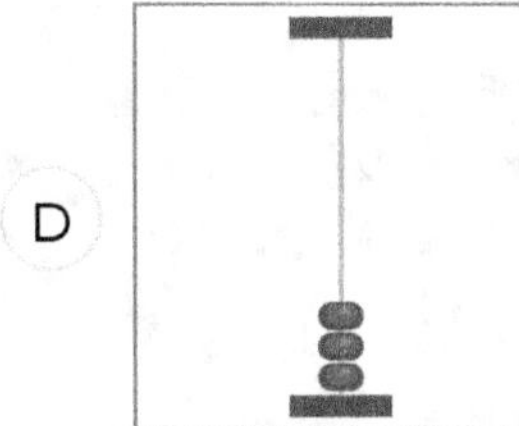

D

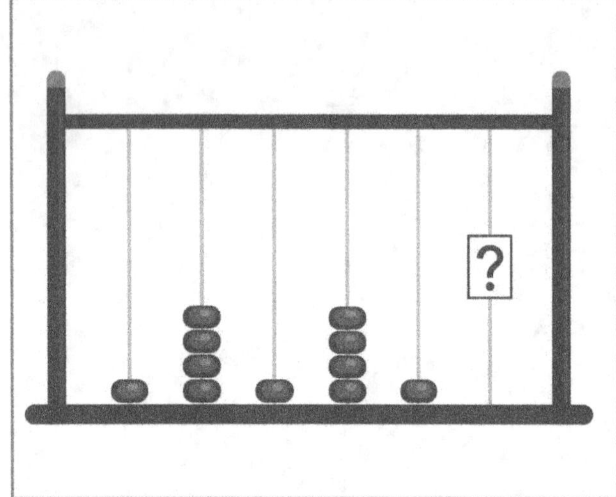

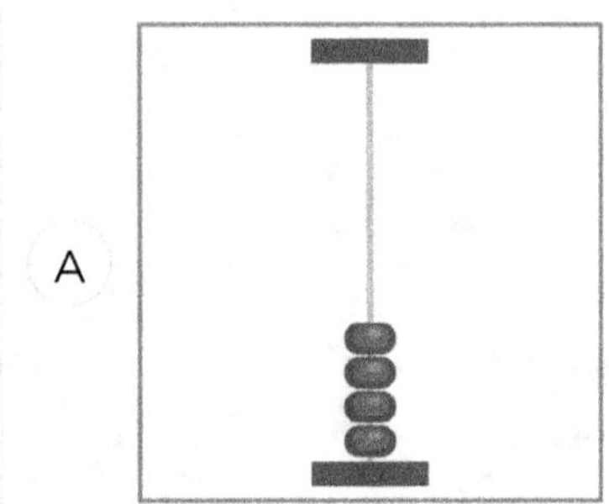

A

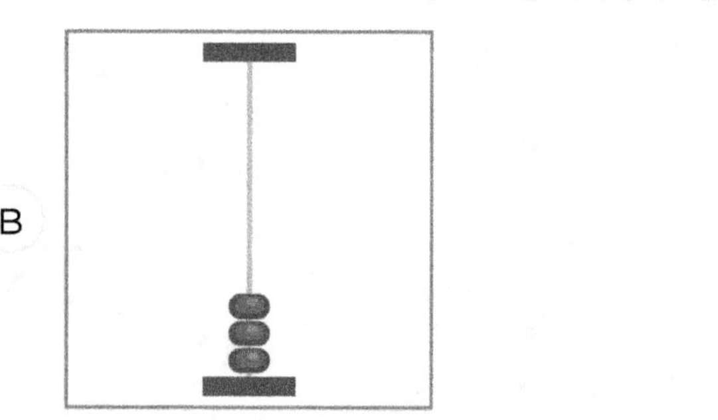

B

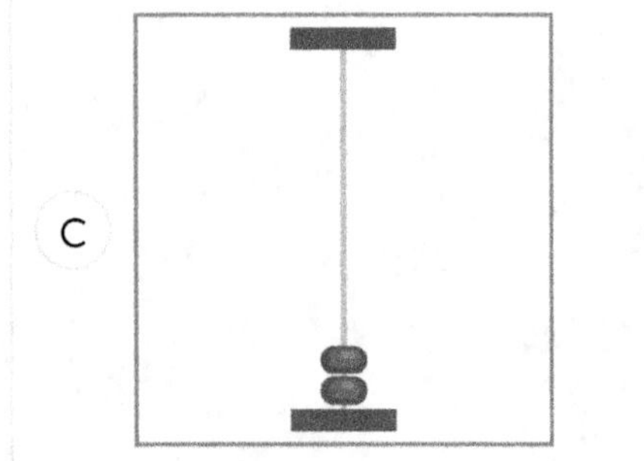

C

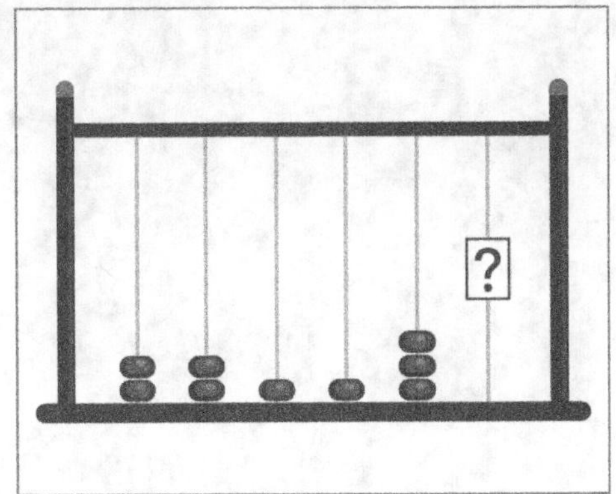

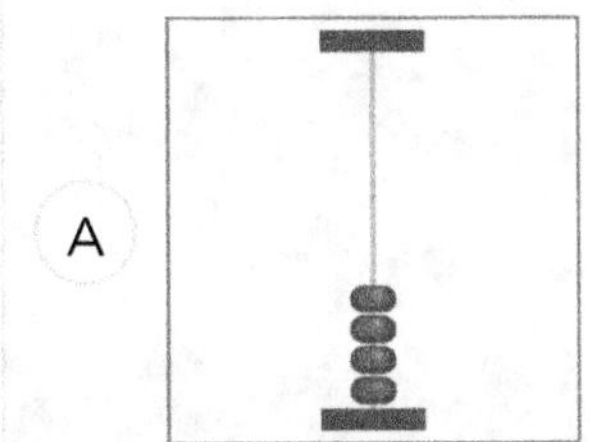

A

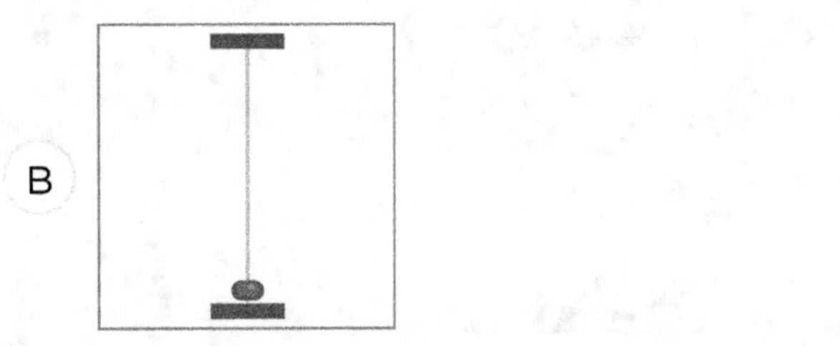

B

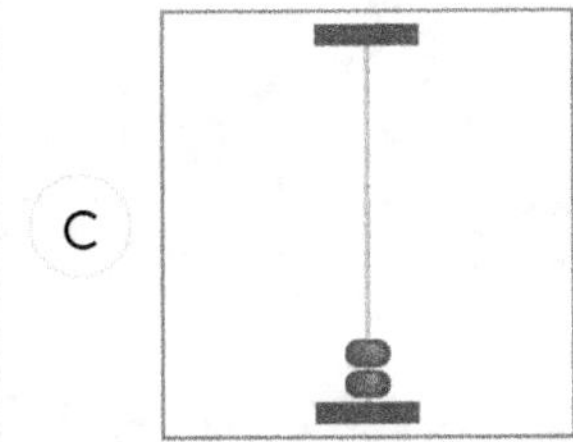

C

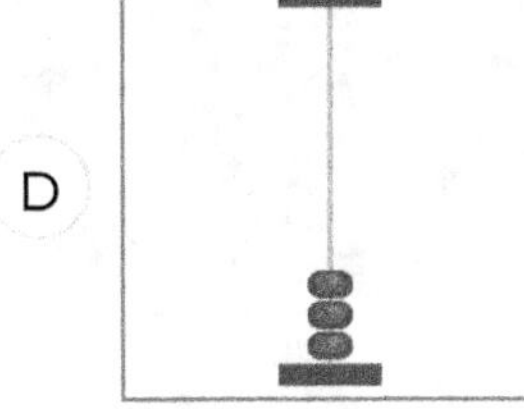

D

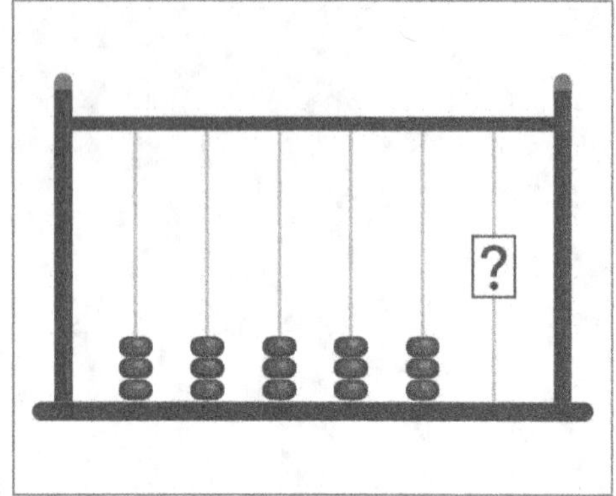

A 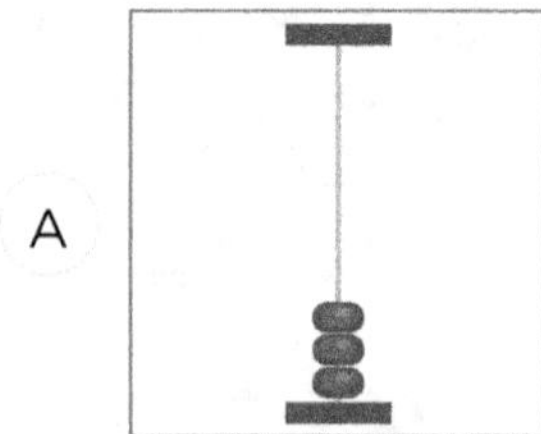

C 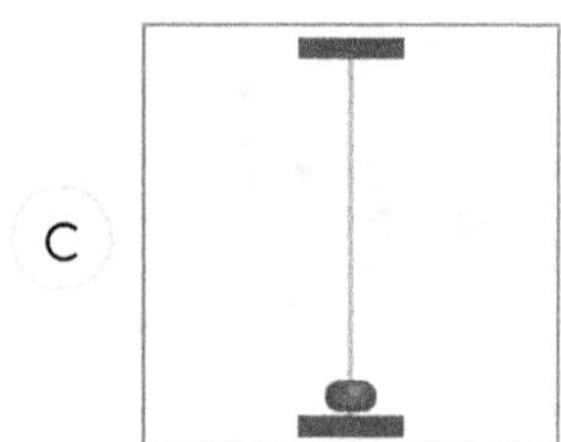

B 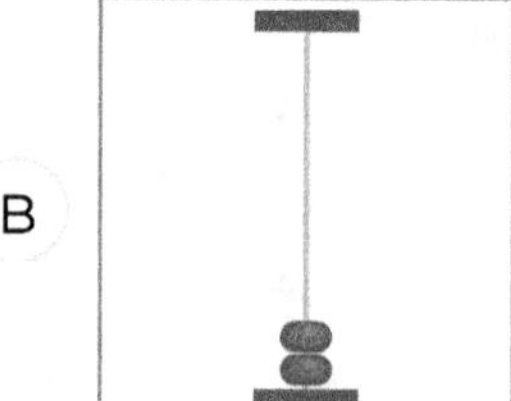

D 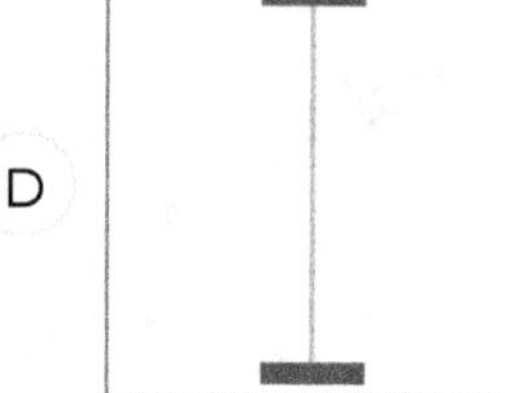

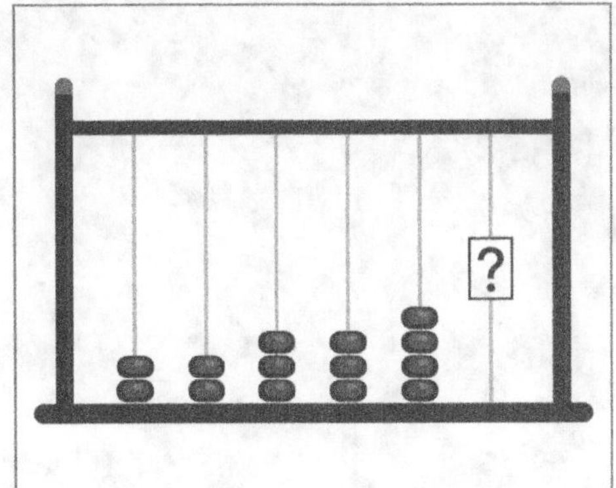

A
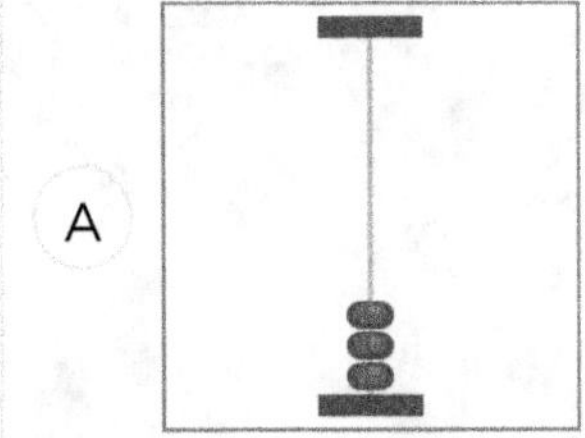

B
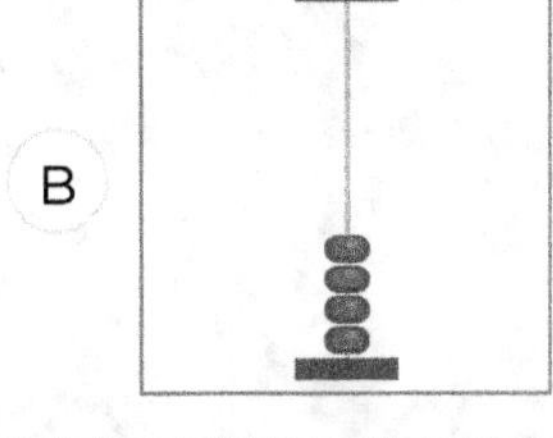

C
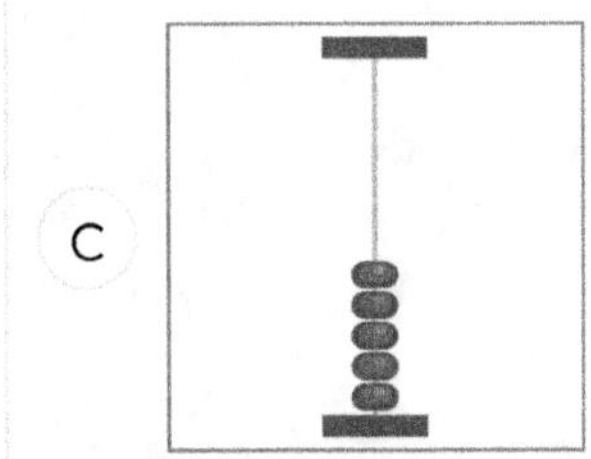

D
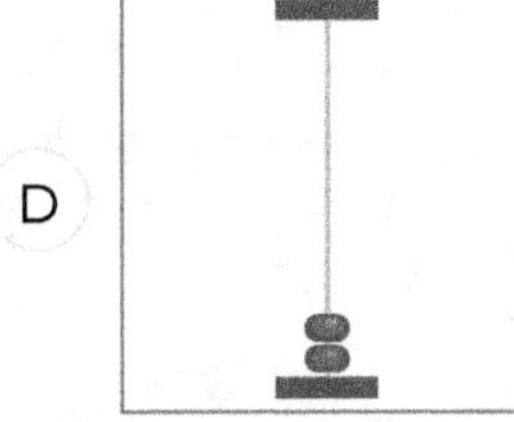

Question 10

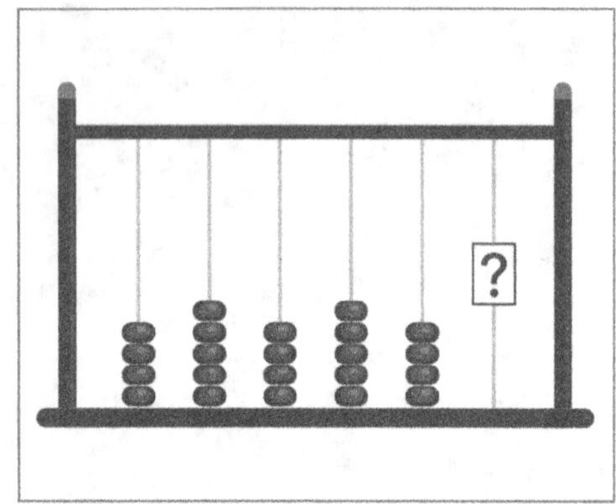

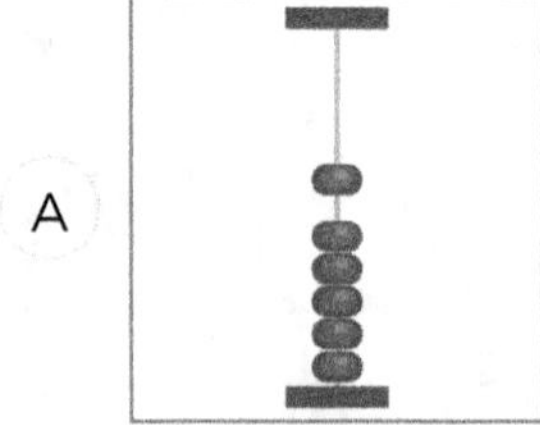

A

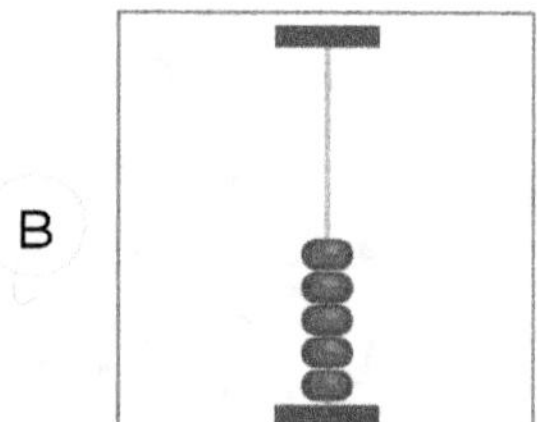

B

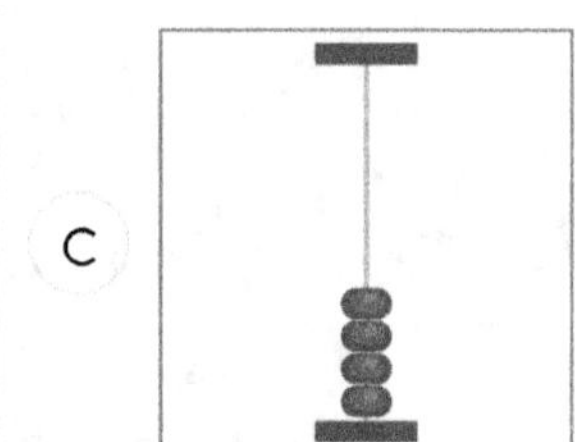

C

1. a
2. a
3. c
4. c
5. c
6. a
7. d
8. a
9. b
10. b

Verbal
Picture Analogies

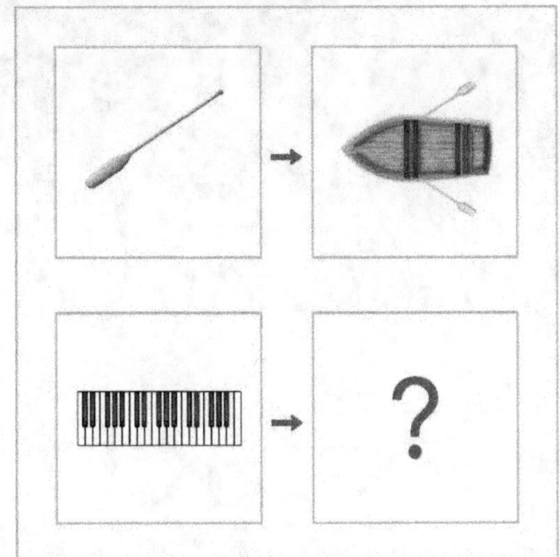

A 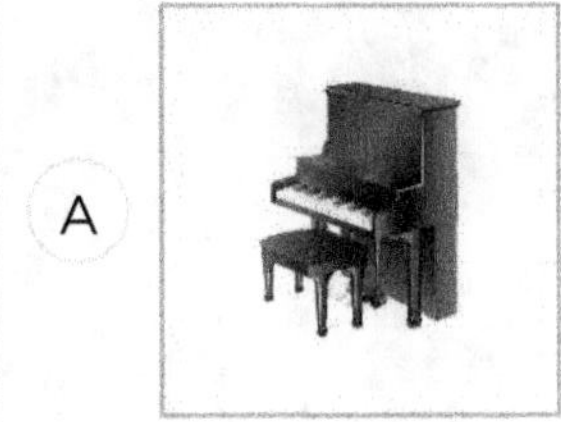

B 

C 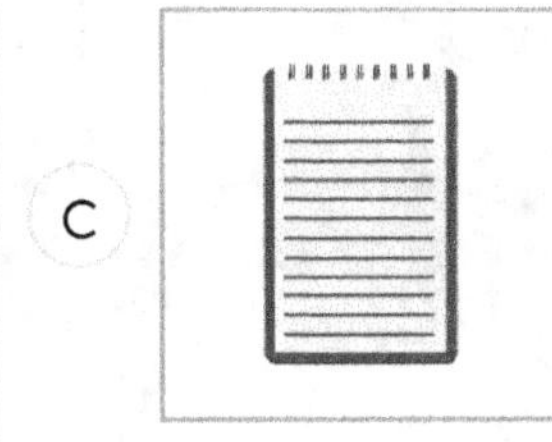

D 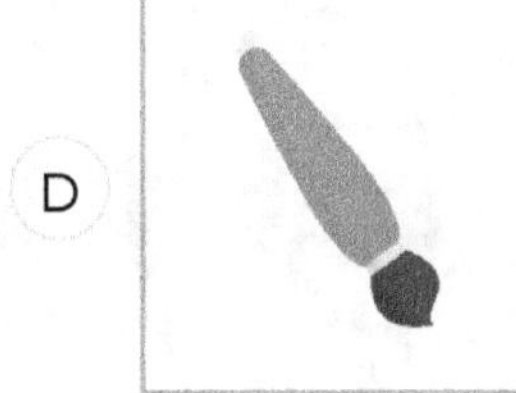

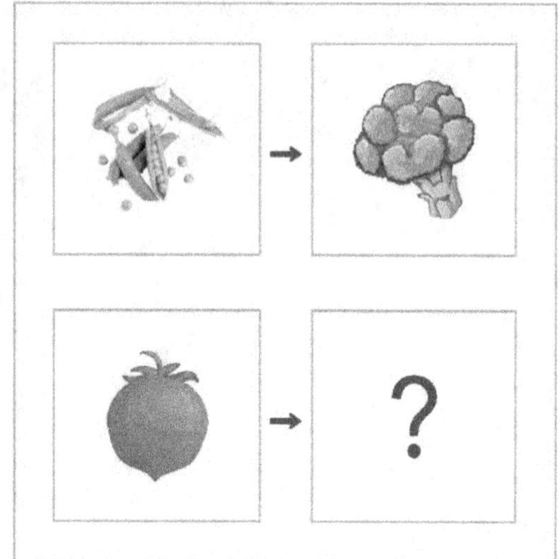

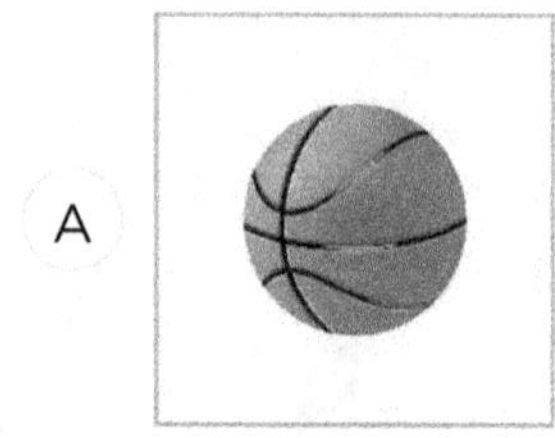

A

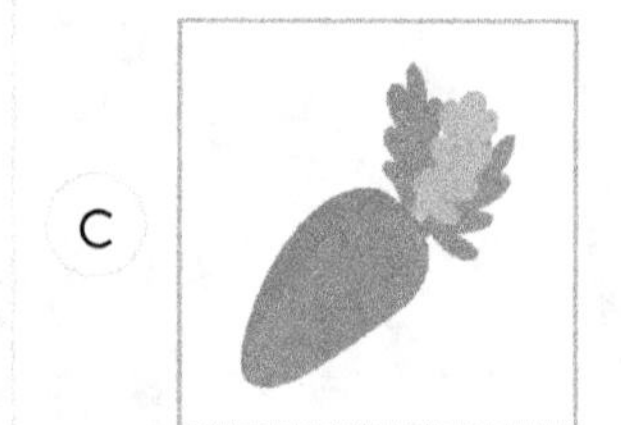

B

C

A

B

C

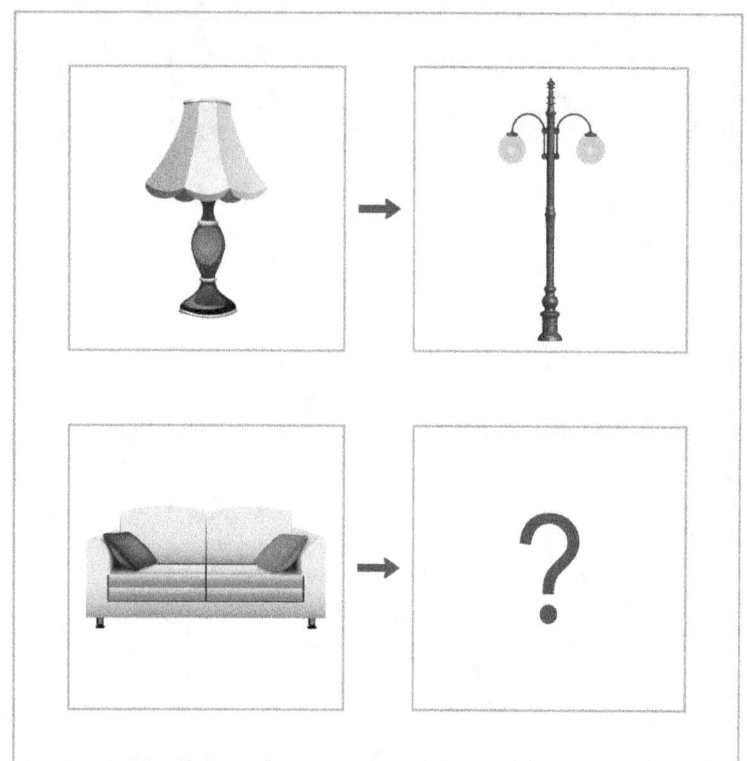

A 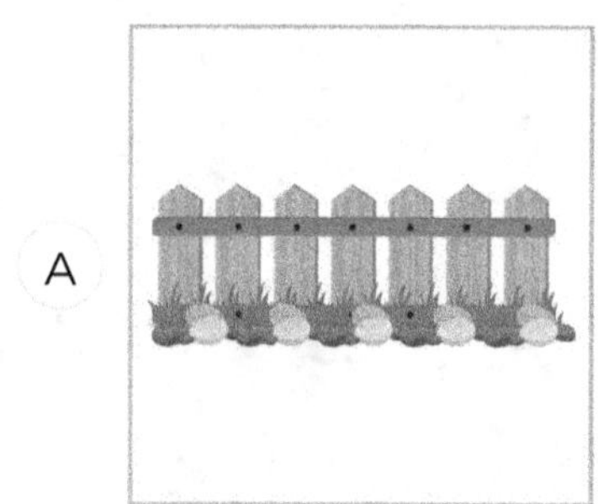

B 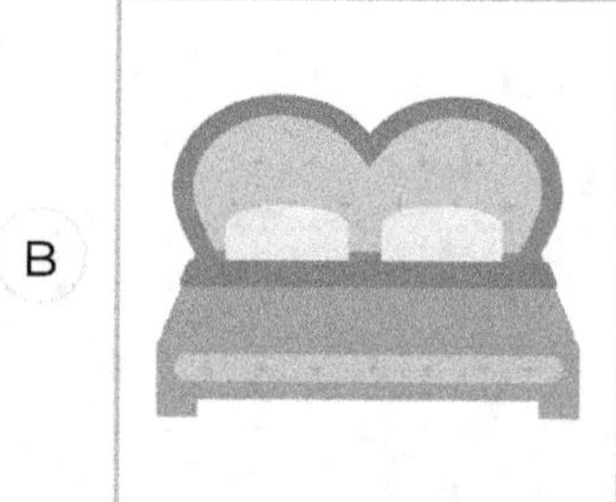

C 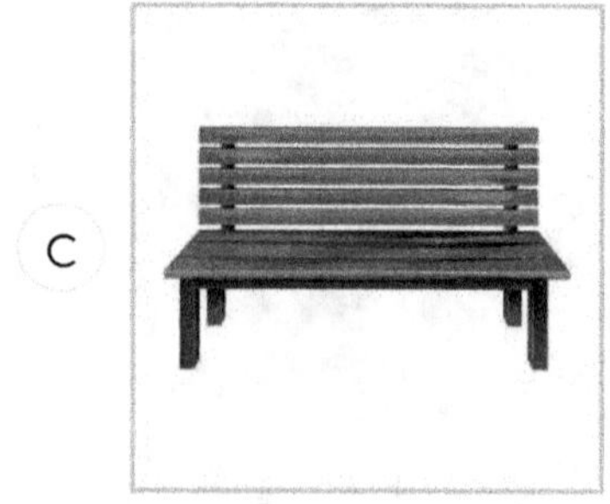

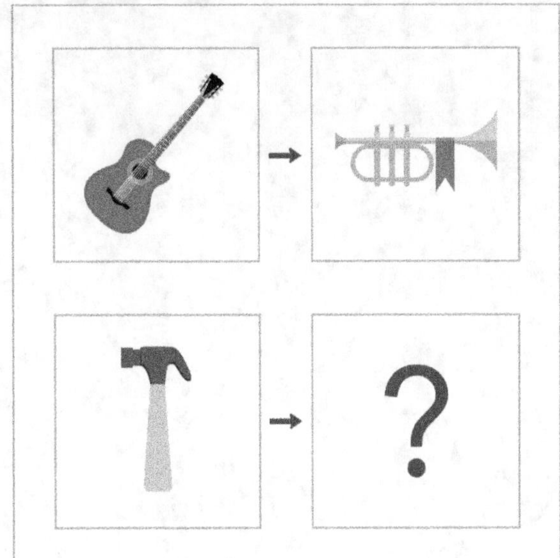

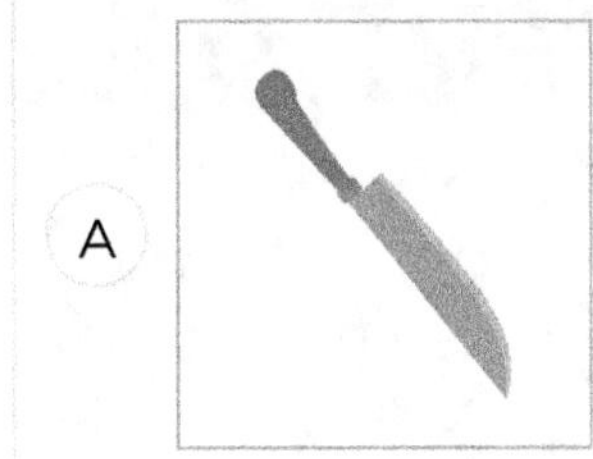

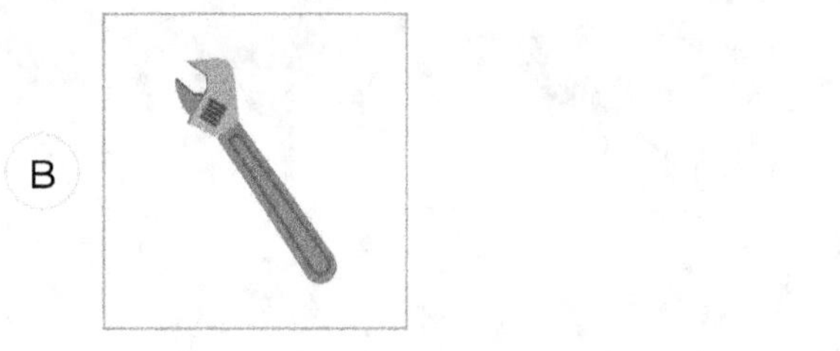

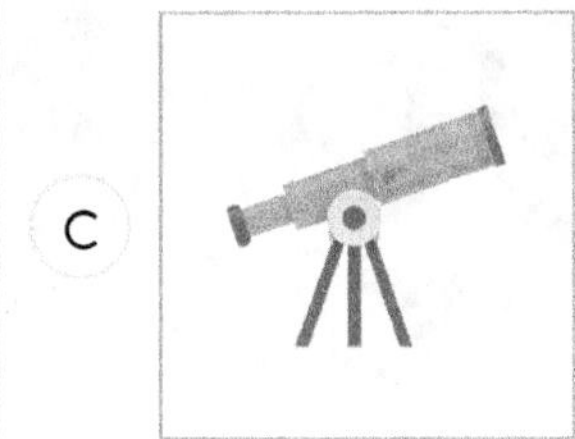

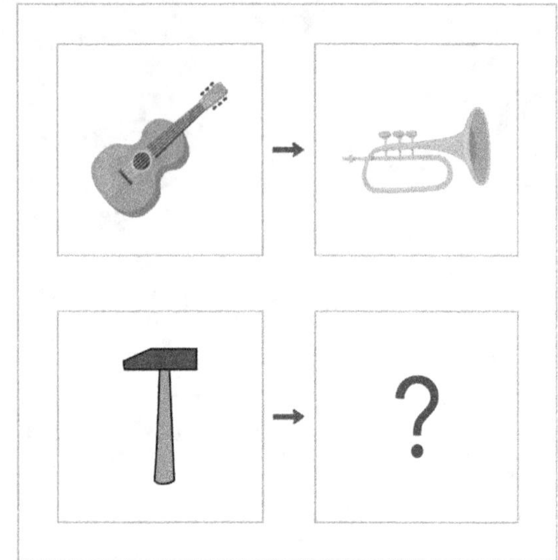

A

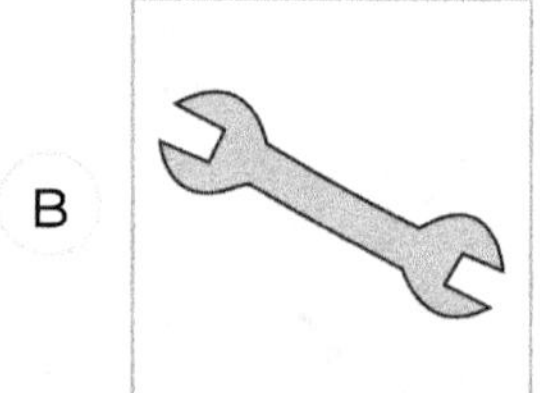

B

C

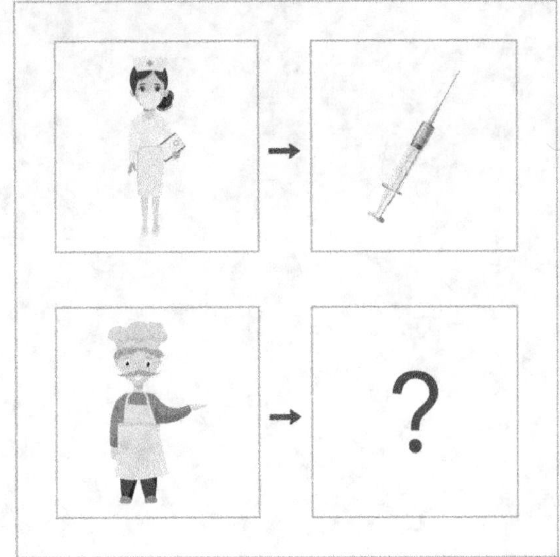

A 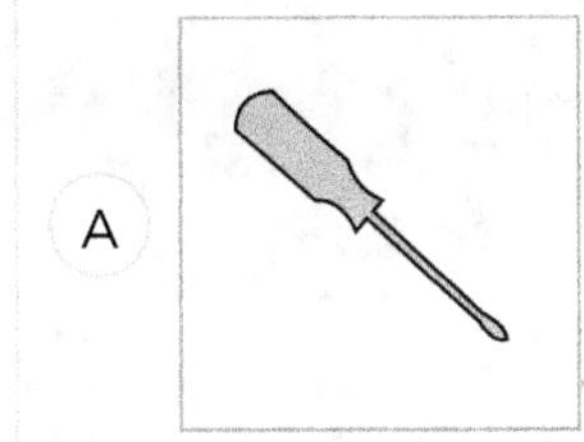

B 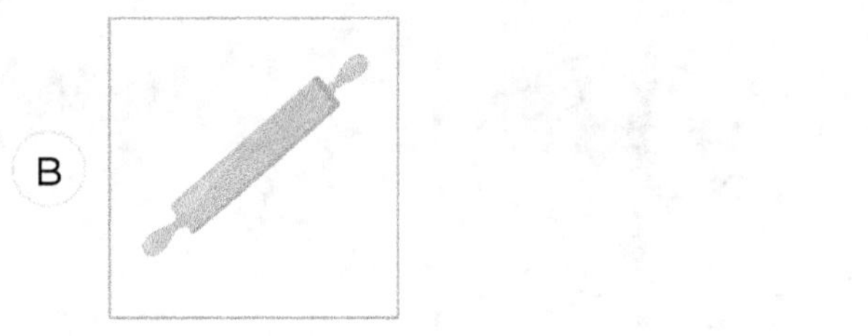

C 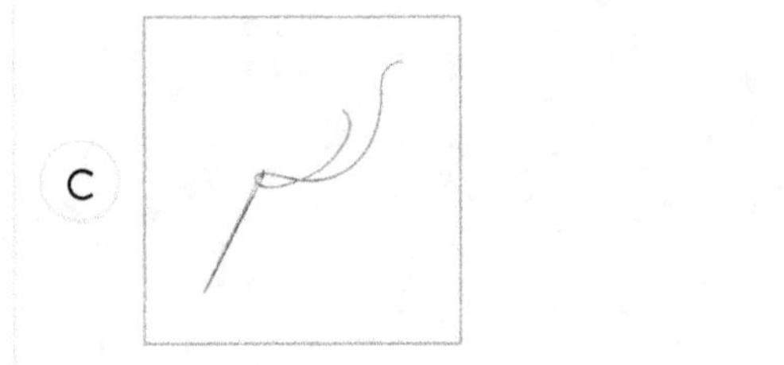

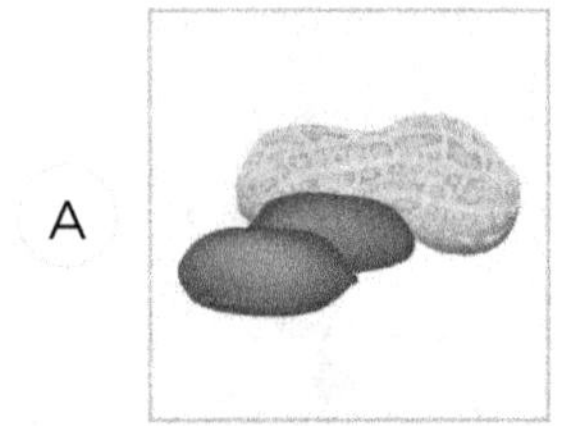

A

B

C

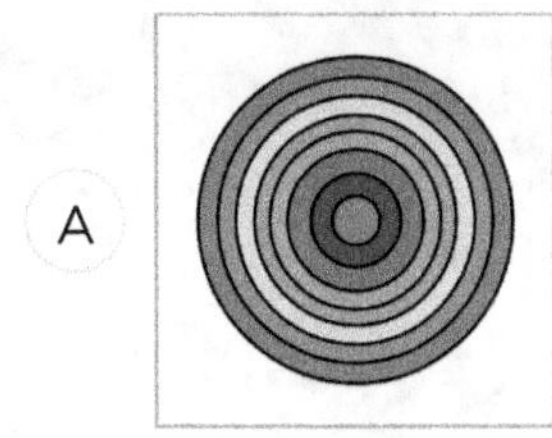

A

B

C

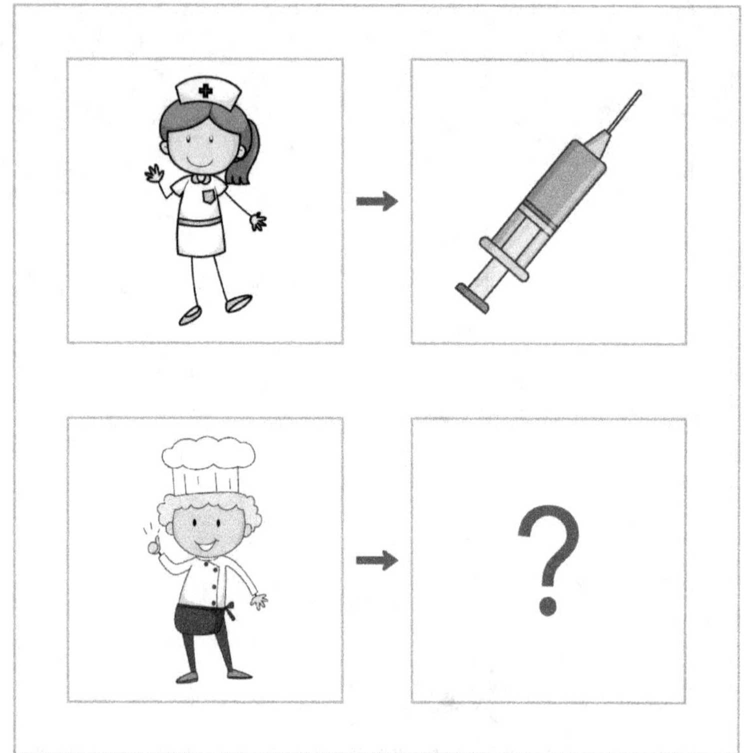

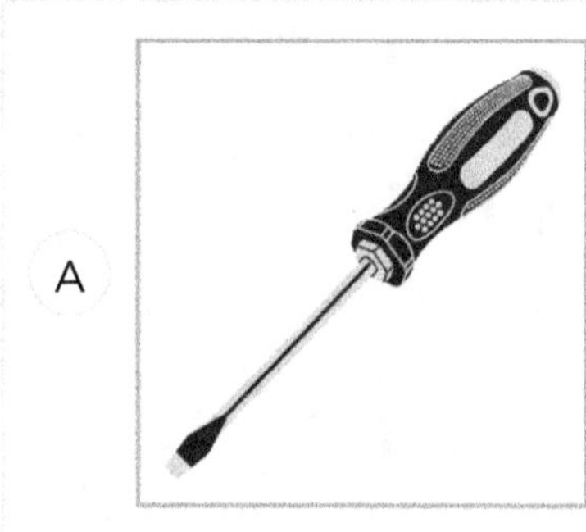

A

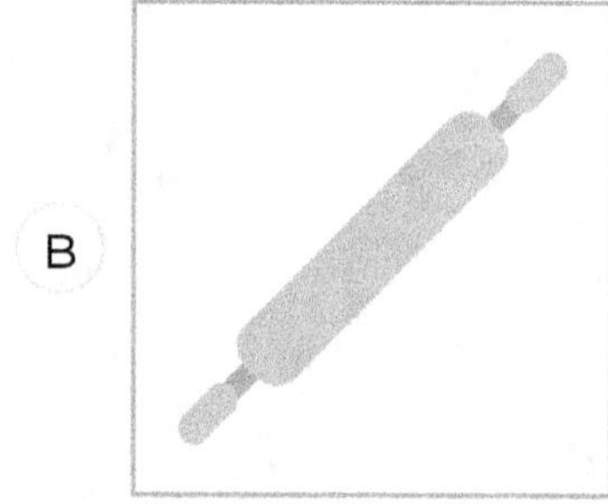

B

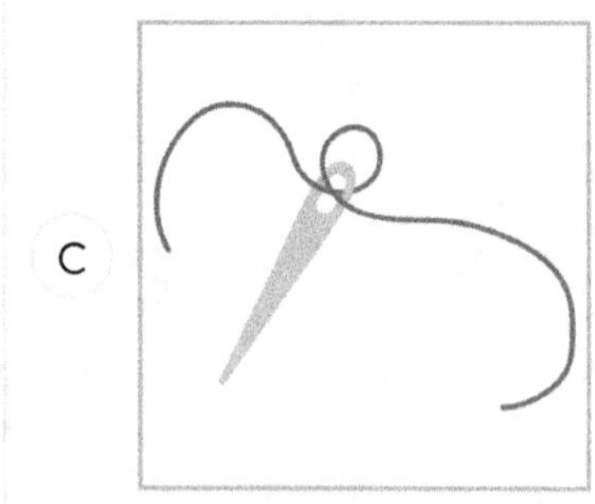

C

1. a
2. c
3. b
4. c
5. b
6. b
7. b
8. c
9. a
10. b

Verbal
Picture Clasification

 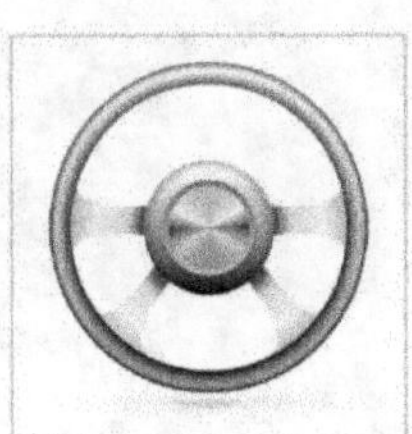 

A 

B 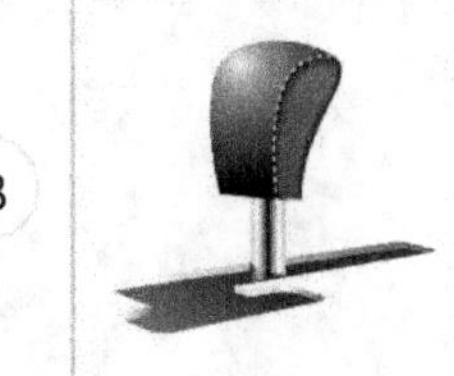

C 

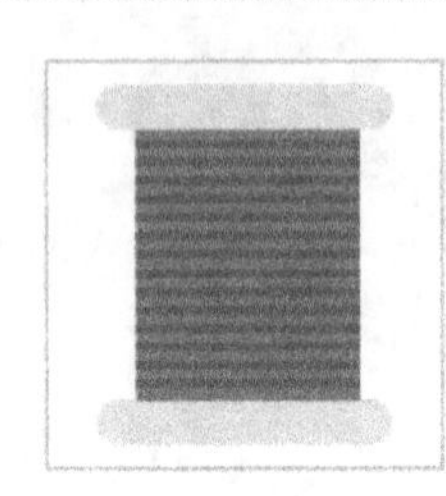  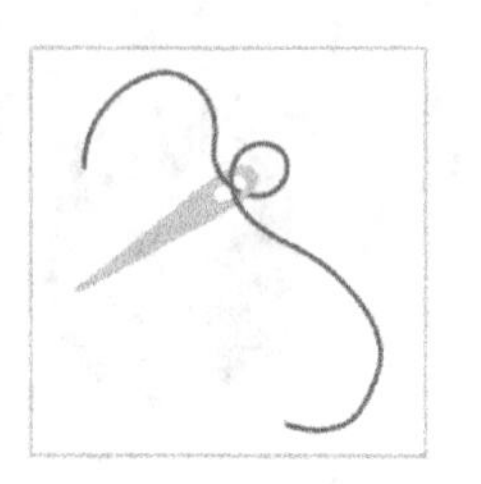

A 

B 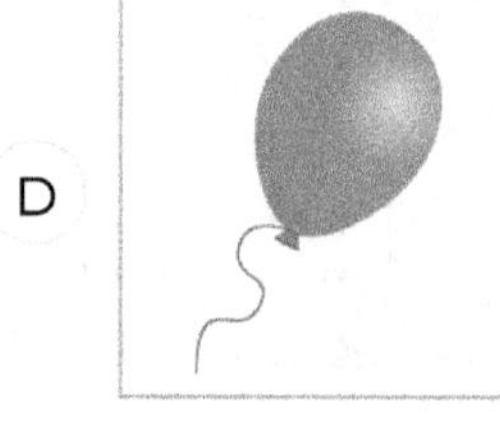

A 

B 

C 

A 

B 

C 

  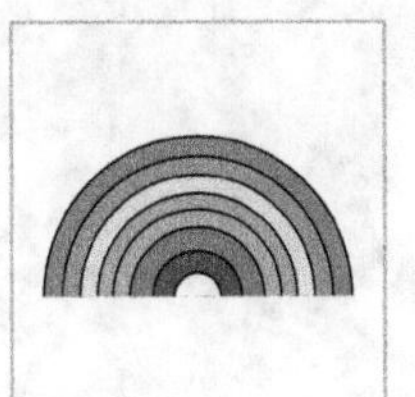

A 

B 

C 

 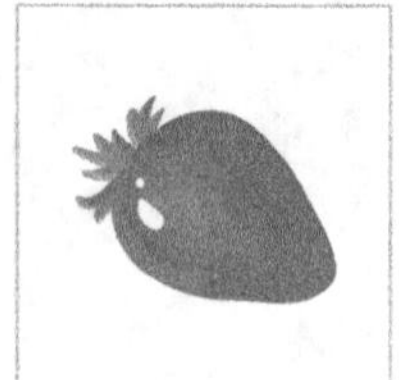 

A 

B 

C 

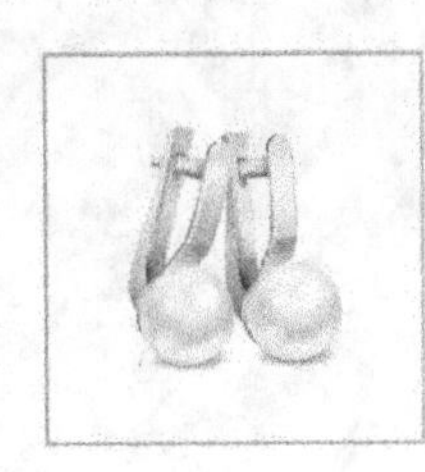  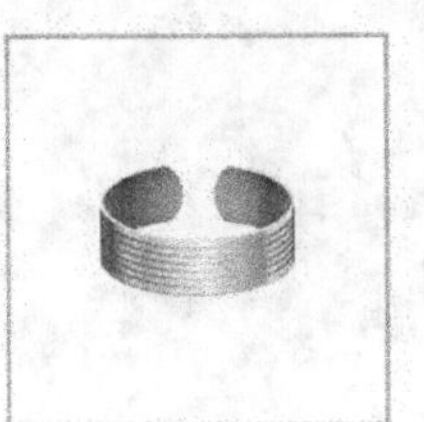

A 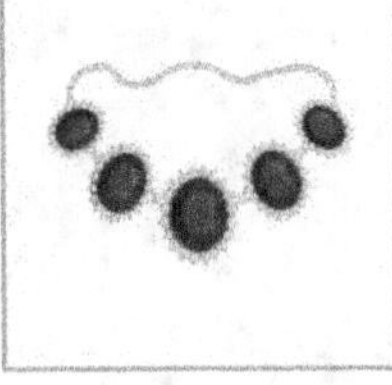

B 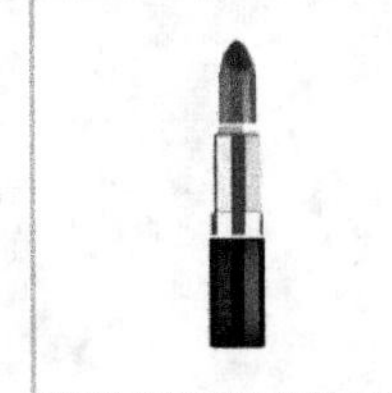

C 

A 

B 

C 

A 

B 

C 

A 

B 

C 

D 

1. b
2. a
3. c
4. a
5. a
6. c
7. a
8. a
9. a
10. c

Verbal
Sentence Completion

Which of these would you use for a front stroke?

A 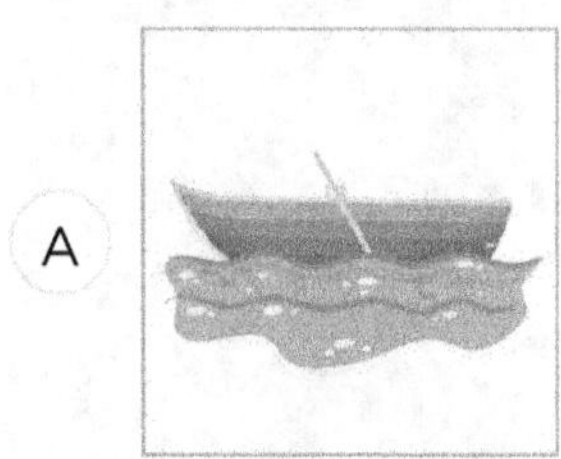

B 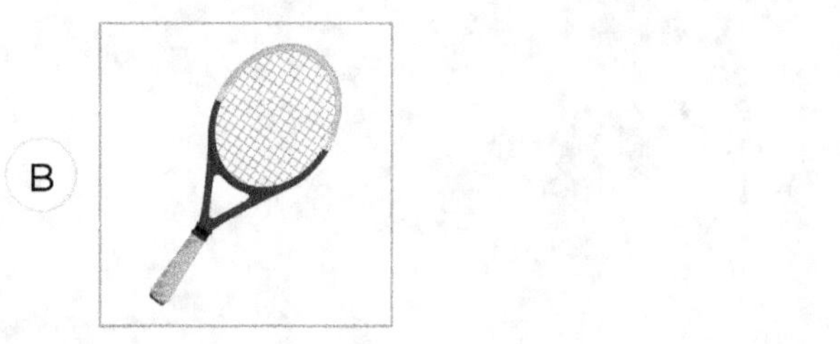

C 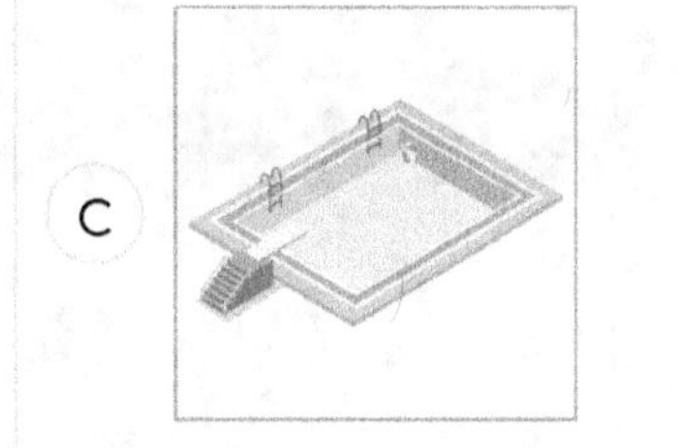

D 

Which of these would a lady use when she is putting on her makeup?

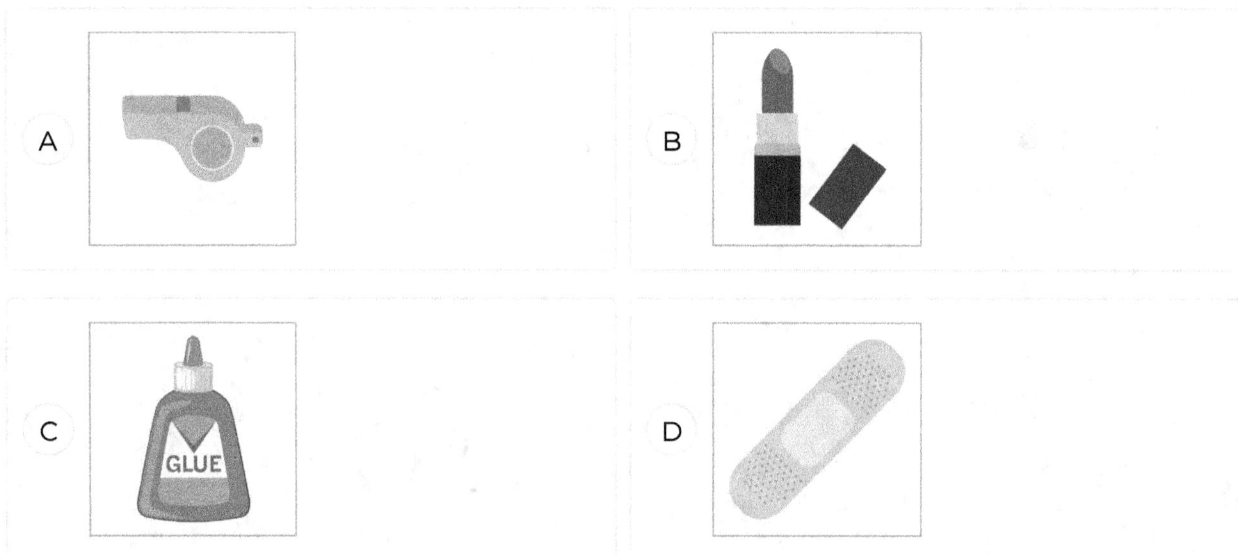

Which of these would you use on a nail?

A 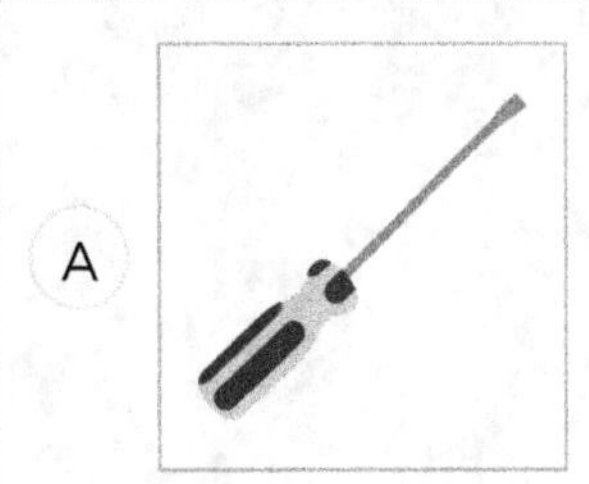

B 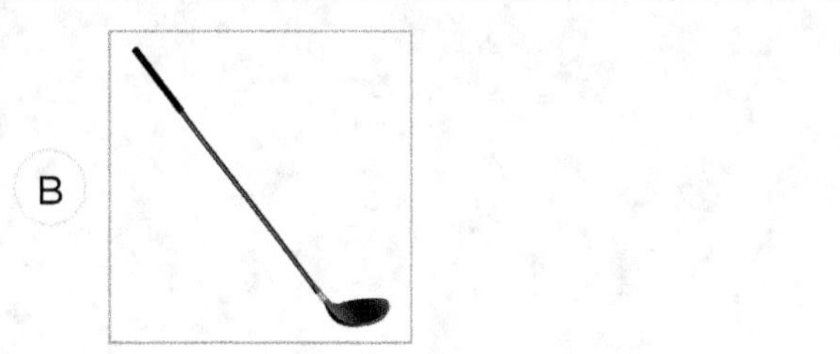

C 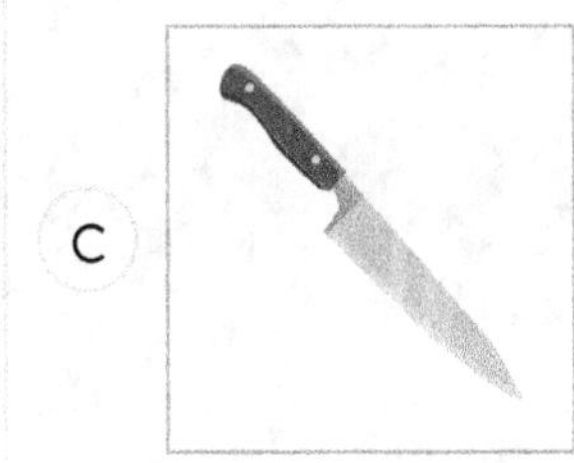

D 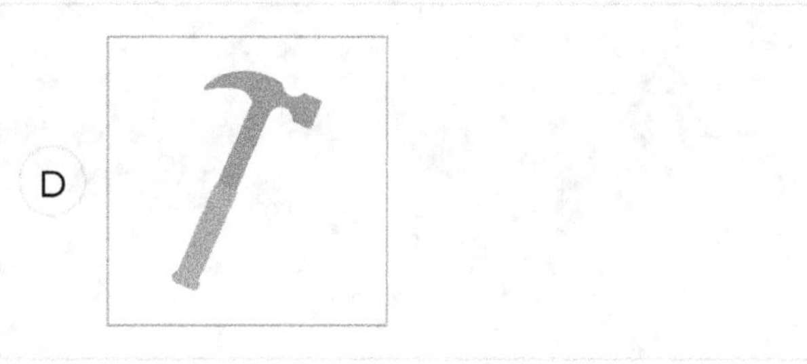

Which of these would you use to figure out on which day of the week your birthday would fall?

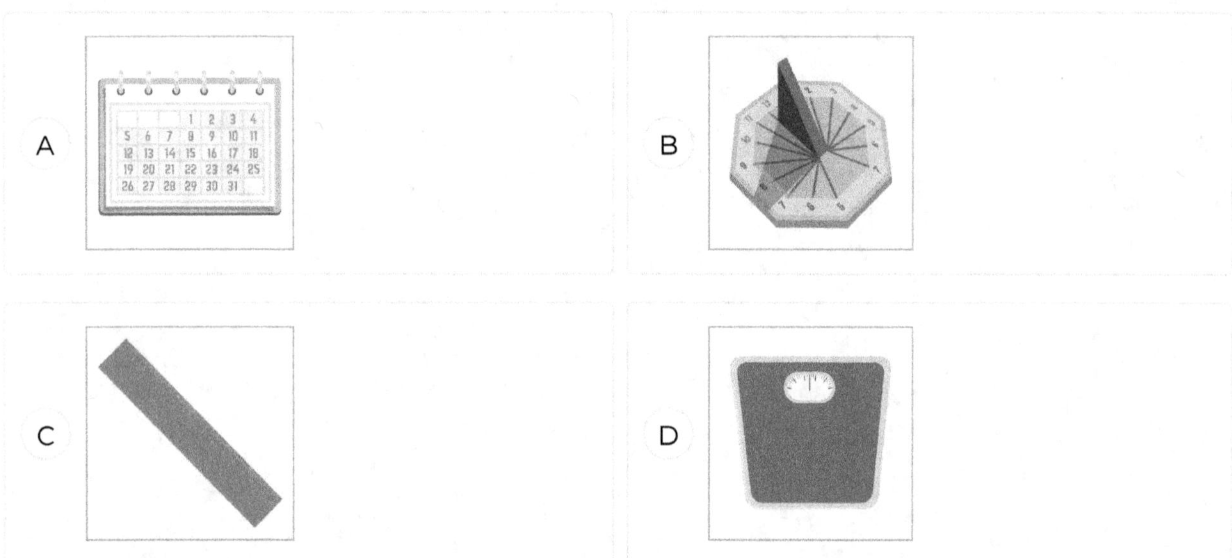

Which of the following objects help to ensure that everyone in an auditorium hears our voice?

A 	B 
C 	D 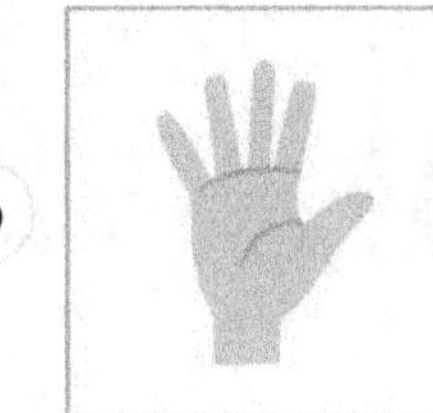
E 	

Which of these would you find in a bathroom?

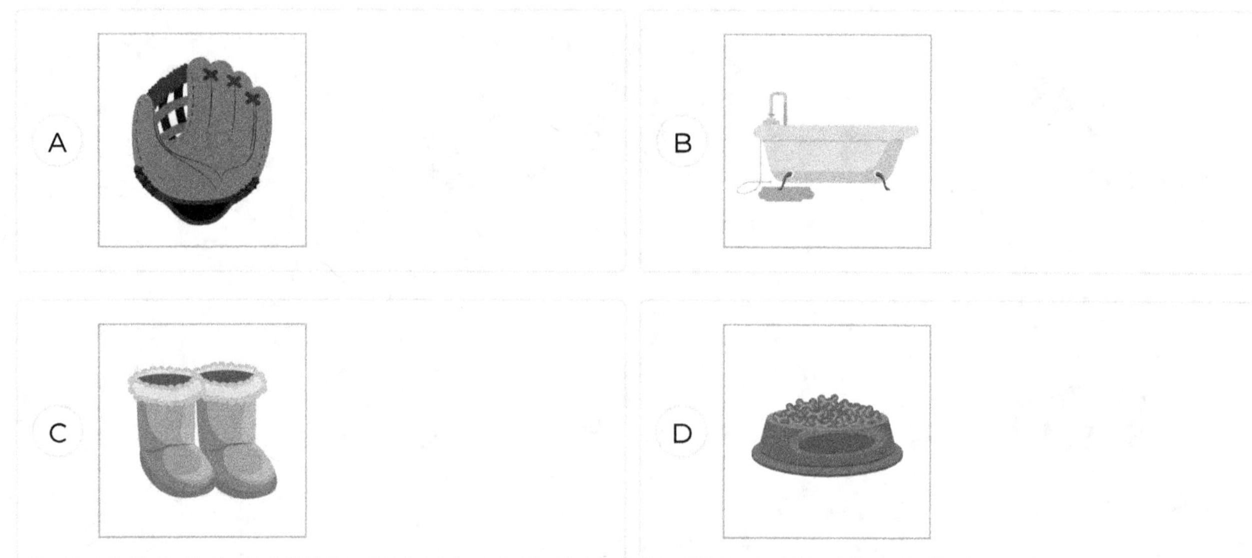

A

B

C

D

Which of these would you need to put together?

A

B

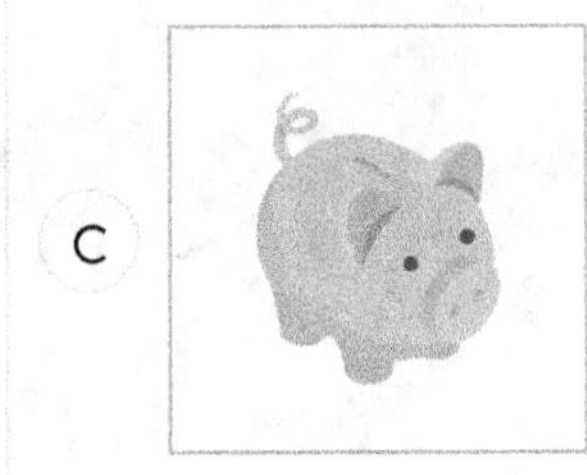

C

D

Which one of the following objects would be used to remove snow?

A
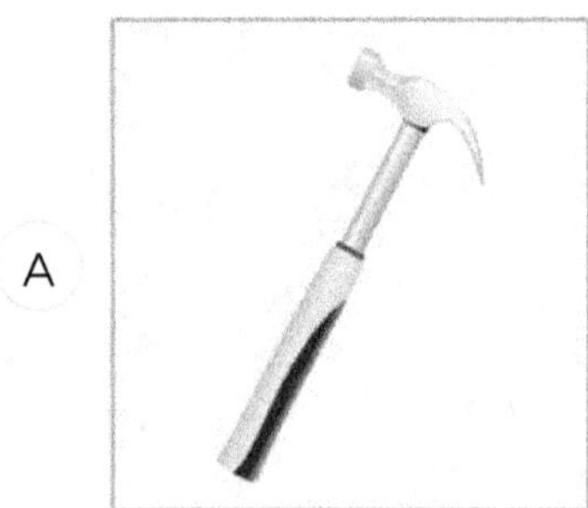

B

C
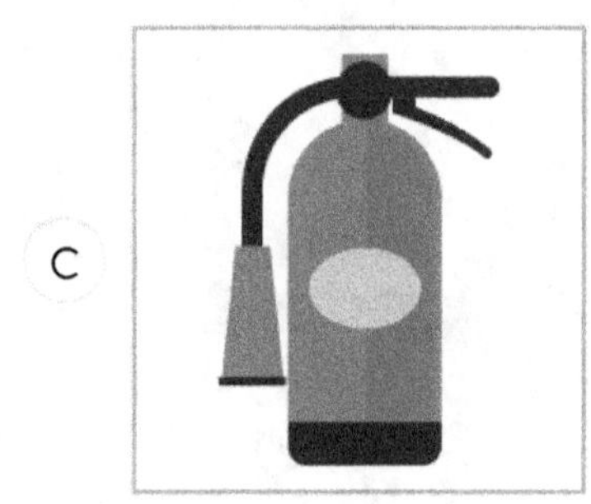

D
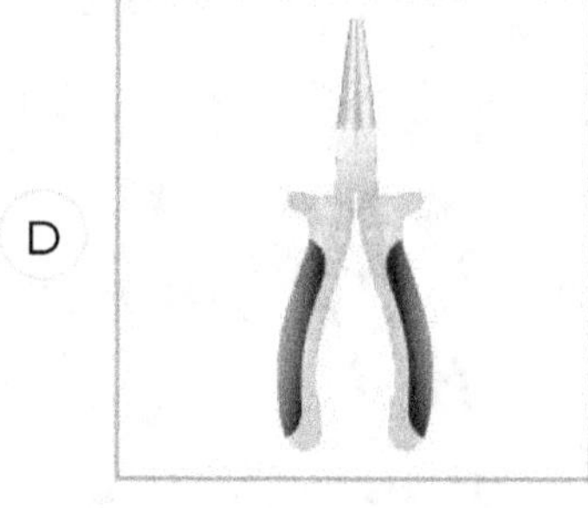

Which of the following objects would you use if you were going on vacation?

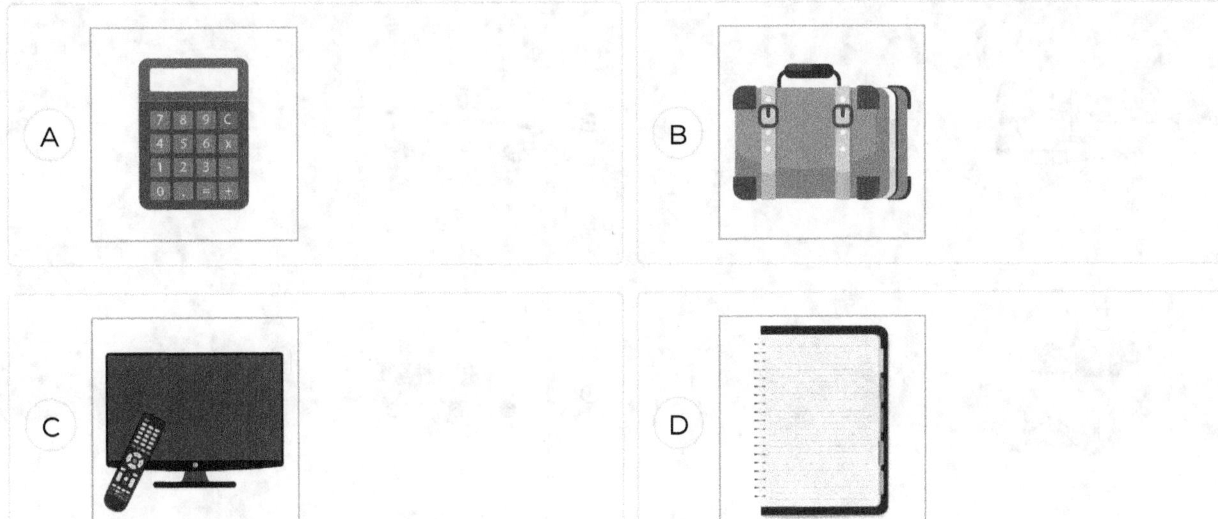

A

B

C

D

Andrew called 911 for a medical emergency. Which one of the following vehicles would arrive?

A 

B 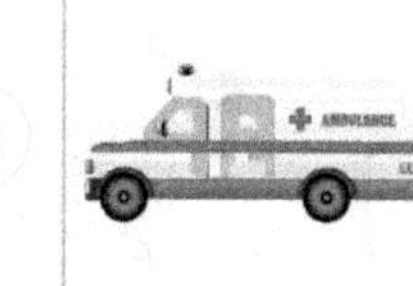

C 

D 

1. c
2. b
3. d
4. a
5. a
6. b
7. d
8. b
9. b
10. b

Explore Other books by Mirvoxid Press

these and more other Test Preps and Study Guides on Amazon Store:

Canada Store:

US Store: